TRUCE:
Ending the Sibling War

TRUCE:

Ending the Sibling War

By Janet Bode

FRANKLIN WATTS
New York/London/Toronto/Sydney/1991

Library of Congress Cataloging-in-Publication Data
Bode, Janet.
Truce : ending the sibling war / by Janet Bode
p.   cm.
Includes bibliographical references and index.
Summary: Explores the sometimes poor relationships of children and teens
with their brothers and sisters, focusing especially on ways to end conflict
and improve relations by changing attitudes and behavior.
ISBN 0-531-15221-9. — ISBN 0-531-10996-8 (lib. bdg.)
1. Sibling rivalry. 2. Brothers and sisters. 3. Sibling rivalry—Case studies. 4.
Brothers and sisters—Case studies. [1. Sibling rivalry. 2. Brothers and
sisters.]   I. Title.
BF723.S43B63   1991
155.44′3—dc20   90—47322 CIP AC

155.44
B

CONTENTS

To my sisters, Barbara and Carolyn, and my stepbrother and stepsister, Tony and Judy

ACKNOWLEDGMENTS

This book would not have been possible without the support of my family and my friends. Special praise goes to: My father and fellow writer, Carl Bode, and my stepmother, Charlotte; my partner, Stan Mack; my friends, Lucy Cefalu, Jeanne Dougherty, Andrea Eagan, Kay Franey, Ted Gottfried, Neil Hedin, Carole Mayedo, Rosemarie and Marvin Mazor, Vince Pravata, and Howie Rosen.

I also received invaluable assistance from these sources: Claudine Jackson, YA Specialist, Kansas City, Missouri, Public Library; Connie Lawson, YA Specialist, Maple Heights, Ohio, Public Library; Marylou Gall, librarian, Milkovich Middle School; Clara Thoren Rottman, Director of Library Media Services, Lincoln, Nebraska, Public Schools; Madeleine Schulps, librarian, Theodore Roosevelt High School, Bronx, New York; Jean Stern, Nancy Chu, and Inga Oppenheimer, librarians,

John Bowne High School, Flushing, New York; Jeanne Vestal and Iris Rosoff, at my publisher, Franklin Watts; and the individual student consultants who volunteered to share their stories.

TO THE READER

Siblings: two or more individuals who have the same parent

When I started to talk to students about how they got along with their sisters and brothers, I expected to hear about such sibling problems as borrowing stuff without asking or arguing about whose turn it was to do the dishes. Well, for some teenagers, those were the issues.

"What's the angriest you ever got at your two older brothers?" I ask a sixteen-year-old jock from Nebraska. He thinks awhile and then answers, "Once after baseball practice they were supposed to pick me up, but they forgot."

Billy, a seventh-grader and a youngest child from Mississippi, gives this example of what, for him, is a major sibling problem: "I pull tricks where I know I'll be babied. Like, I've been known to yell, 'Ow, quit hitting me!' to try to get my brother in trouble and to test how fast my mom will run to save me. Lately she just loafs in and she won't even tell him to go to his room."

Fourteen-year-old Melinda has twin siblings, one of whom really embarrasses her: "My brother never takes a bath unless my parents holler. He sleeps in his clothes and then the next day he wears them to school. *Blech!*"

I ask these students what benefits they find in having brothers and sisters. For many, the answers come quickly. Ganeen, eighteen, from Oregon, laughs about the night her younger brother dressed up in a wig and lipstick to crash her girls-only slumber party. A Maryland fifteen-year-old, one of five kids, mentions that she and her fourteen-year-old sister are so close they "can read each other's mind." A Vermont seventeen-year-old says she is always glad to have older siblings to "break in my parents."

All these teenagers recognize that the difficulties they have with their siblings are routine aggravations—part of any daily, close contact. Sure, their brothers and sisters can sometimes be a giant pain, but they don't hate them. And especially, they don't fear them.

But about every fourth student, however, the stories that unfold are far different. What they speak about are lives in crisis.

For example, Ann shows up for her interview with a broken arm. The night before she got into a "disagreement" with her sixteen-year-old brother. When he saw a blemish on her neck, he accused her of fooling around with her boyfriend. He didn't like that. To make his point, he pushed her. Hard. "I hit against a dresser, my arm kind of flew back and a mirror fell down," says this eighteen-year-old.

14

A junior from Illinois says that in her family, fighting words are just that. Fighting is the way they communicate with each other. Robert, a fifteen-year-old from New Jersey, describes his home as a "door-slamming household." They scream at each other and then when they "have nothing better to say," they walk out and *Blam!*— slam the door behind them. Another fifteen-year-old, this one from Hawaii, keeps postponing our phone conversation. Both her parents work, and she's the full-time baby-sitter for her younger siblings.

These teenagers—the 25 percent—say they wake up each day feeling angry, confused, and trapped. And they go to bed at night feeling the same way. Most of them also share one other feeling: they don't want to give up. They want to make their family life better. The catch is that they don't have any idea how to go about doing that.

If you have serious sibling problems, this book will remind you that you're not alone. And I hope it will help you change your relationships into happy and supportive ones.

As you read this book, you'll come to parts in boxes like the one around these words. Inside the boxes will be the stories of teenagers spoken in their own words about problems in their lives. The language isn't always perfect. The emotions may be confused. They are, though, the voices of kids living under considerable pressure in complicated family situations.

The students who agreed to share their experiences asked that their privacy be protected. To conceal their identities, I changed their names and a few other details. The events, the emo-

tions, and the sense of what they've been going through are absolutely real.

Panel of Experts

After interviewing the teenagers, I turned to adult sources, experts whose jobs are to help others understand and resolve difficulties. Throughout this book, you'll see various references to these "experts." Listed at the back of the book on page 102 is background information about the men and women who answer your questions and offer solutions to sibling problems.

1

RUNNING ON EMPTY

> *"My brother Darnell—he's thirteen—he cursed at me, called me a female dog. I got real mad. So I hit him and made his nose bleed. I fought him and fought him," says fifteen-year-old Cherisse.*
>
> *"Yeah, she was beating me up bad," Darnell agrees. "So I went to the kitchen and picked up a big knife. I threw it at her. She ducked. There it was, sticking in the wall."*

What words describe how sisters and brothers are supposed to act with each other? There's "mothering" and "fathering," but no "sistering" and "brothering." The rules you hear are usually vague: Behave yourselves, don't fight, and look after your little brother—instructions that can mean very different things, depending on the family.

How step-, half-, and foster sibling relationships should work is even fuzzier. Is the idea to treat one another like real brothers and sisters, whatever that means? Or do you act more like friends? Cousins? Neighbors?

While no one—not you or the experts—can easily come up with answers to these questions, you know when things in your home aren't right. You know when there's nonstop arguing or fights that end in physical violence. You know if you're being forced to be a parent, when you're really still a child. Do you hide your stuff because a brother or sister steals from you? Has normal sexual curiosity among your siblings gotten out of hand? Are you or is a sibling emotionally out of control?

If you recognize any of these situations, welcome to the harsh world of reality. That's how some brothers and sisters treat each other. For many teenagers, the story is the same: their home life is lousy. For others, it's even worse: they're in physical and emotional danger.

Meanwhile, you flip on the TV to watch those idealized family shows. There's Alex and Mallory, Theo and Vanessa. But you know what you see on that box is *not* what's going on inside your own home. Compare your family experiences with "Family Ties" and "The Cosby Show," and you know your life isn't like that. It may seem to you that those half-hour dilemmas with snap solutions are the closest you'll ever come to any sibling fun.

Now here is a fact: Sibling relationships come with rough edges. You wouldn't be human if every now and then you didn't get mad at a sister or brother. I talked to experts. Of these psychiatrists, psychologists, therapists, social workers, school counselors, mediation specialists, and scientists, all but the only children admitted that when *they* were growing up, they, too, had tough moments with their sisters and brothers.

Within our borders and around the world, you find accounts of sibling problems in the oldest written records and oral traditions. In every nation on earth, there are stories of families fighting. As long as there have been families, clans, and tribes, one child has battled against another.

What seems to be different today is the numbers.

I made a random survey of teenagers in Annapolis, Maryland; Pascagoula, Mississippi; San Diego, California; and in major cities in between. In classroom groups and in one-on-one phone conversations, I talked with middle, junior, and senior high school students. Some of them came from intact families where they'd lived with the same mother and father "forever." Others lived with a parent or an adult in charge who seemed "to change partners as often as light bulbs," as one student put it. What these teenagers called home varied, too, from a farmhouse in the country where the nearest neighbor was a five-minute walk to a cramped two-room apartment in a tenement-filled section of the Bronx in New York City.

Afterward, I went over all the interviews. I found that almost one out of four of these teenagers told about having serious difficulties with siblings. They felt caught in painful, confusing situations that they couldn't understand. You may be part of that 25 percent. If so, this book is for you.

"I hate my sisters, and they hate each other,"
says fifteen-year-old Bonnie, when asked how
she likes being the youngest of four kids. "I can

19

*hardly wait for them to all leave and then I'll
be the only one left. I'll almost be an only child.*

"*My oldest sister, Maxine, she's twenty-one
now and out of the house. Back when she was
younger, she had a really, really bad temper.
She beat on me with her fists. She yelled at me.
I just couldn't stand it; I cried all the time. She
terrified me.*

"*My other two sisters, Debbie and Christine,
punched me, too. One burned me with a curling
iron. The other one pushed me against the hot
stove. It still happens sometimes, but now I can
protect myself better.*

"*Where are my parents when this is happening? My dad's very busy being a lawyer. He's
gone a lot. Once when he was here, Maxine
threw him against the wall. Usually my mom is
at home. She doesn't work. Her specialty is
avoiding problems. If she hears the commotion,
she never comes in and says 'quit it' or 'go to
your rooms.' Nobody ever gets punished after
one of our fights. My mother even leaves us
alone if Debbie, the Perfect Child, the one who's
a year older than me, tells her to.*

"*Sometimes I pretend that my mom says to
us,* 'You cannot hit people. *It's out of the ques-
tion. People who do that are wrong. And bad!'*

"*Instead, the most she says is she can't understand how come we fight. She tells us when she
and her sister were growing up, they got along
real well. My dad says he never got along with
his two younger brothers. Now they only see
each other at weddings and funerals. I plan to
only show up for the funerals.*"

2

TESTING GROUND

In the United States, 80 percent of you have at least one brother or sister.[1] When you add to that a stepsibling or two, the percentage shoots still higher. Here's the point. How you get along with each other matters. It matters a lot—and not just for the peace of the household.

For most people, your sisters and brothers serve as the natural testing ground where you first practice how to play, how to share, and how to love. The give and take of future relationships with friends, teachers, bosses, dates, even the guy behind the counter at McDonald's is first tried out with your siblings. How you act in this home-made laboratory helps shape who you are as a person and who you will be in the years to come.

Your relationship with your sister or brother is one of the most important you will have in your life. Starting with Sigmund Freud, the father of psychoanalysis, experts in the field have been intrigued by the subject. For years they've studied and analyzed and debated the nature of this special bond.

Darnell

How do the teenagers I talked to feel about their lives? Darnell, a student who's constantly fighting with his sisters, shrugs and answers, "I feel like I miss the point." On the surface, he's a cocky freshman, rugged and stylish, with a double diamond pattern shaved on the back of his head. He comes on all rap and confidence. Dark-skinned girls, that's what he likes; and mean male friends. He mentions a father and three half brothers. They live two miles away. He never sees them. "So what," says Darnell.

The conversation slows down when he brings up the last eight months. He hasn't been living with his mother. He and his two half sisters—they all have the same mother—have been staying at their grandmother's, along with an uncle and a couple of cousins. Before that, they lived with their mother. That ended two years ago, June 14th. Darnell knows the exact date. You see, he says, that was the day they had to move out of the shelter, a hotel where the city stored homeless families.

Darnell doesn't want to offer many details about the shelter. He doesn't want to talk about why he isn't living with his mother. All he says is that he *isn't* a kid anymore. When he was, he wanted to be another Eddie Murphy. Now he wonders if he'll make it to eighteen. He says his neighborhood echoes with gunshots.

Darnell feels angry a lot, and willing to fight anyone and everyone at the slightest challenge. And he wishes he didn't have so many headaches. But then, there are different kinds of feelings that he holds on to. Last week, his older sister, Cherisse, asked *him* for advice.

"Cherisse said, say she got raped, right, and found out she was pregnant. Should she keep the baby? She thought, yes. I thought, no. 'What if that baby grows up looking just like the rapist? What if the baby gets older and asks where his daddy is?' We talked back and forth and it helped her and made me feel better, too."

Bonnie

How does Bonnie, blond and pretty, feel about herself and her life? Does she feel she's working her way toward independence? "Don't make me laugh," she responds. She feels stuck, ugly, and not very loved. She guesses she's supposed to consider herself lucky, because she comes from an intact family—Mom, Dad, and the kids. She hears her friends from divorced families talk, saying, "bad things about their father to their mother and about their mother to their father."

She tries to forget about the violence her older sister Maxine's done to her, but it's hard to pretend that the real and emotional scars aren't there. This sophomore has had two dates total. She worries, will she ever be popular? Will anybody notice the bruises from her last fight with her sister? She worries so much that her stomach hurts. She has trouble sleeping, and when she wakes up at three in the morning, she worries that people think her family is weird. During lunch hour in a field near school, her sister, Christine, practices satanic rituals. When Christine comes back to class, dressed as usual all in black, she races up and down the hallways shrieking.

Debbie, the sister Bonnie refers to as the Perfect Child, steals from her. It began at Christmas when she swiped a brand new outfit from Bonnie's closet. When caught wearing it, she lied. Oh, I got this at K-Mart,

23

Debbie said, even though she always claims she'll never set foot in that store. Today the Perfect Child, chubby and teased by the other students, refuses to speak to Bonnie. Bonnie says if you want to know the truth about how she feels, numb comes to mind.

Jocelyn

To those who don't know Jocelyn, she seems to have it together. She can go on forever about externals, like fashion and jewelry. She loves getting dressed up and changing her hair style. For her part-time job at a clothing store, she wears heels, a skirt, and a sweater, but never rhinestone accessories, she's fast to add. Right now she describes her hair as light brown in a neat ponytail. Tomorrow, after she uses henna, it'll be auburn and super curly.

What about Jocelyn's life so far? Well, she never wanted a sibling in the first place, and if she had to have one, she wanted an older brother. She likes motorcross rides and watching football. With a big brother to lead, she'd be able to play what she calls the little-sister role. Also, an older brother would "go after and kill" anyone who was causing her trouble. And maybe an older brother would make her feel less insecure. Once she convinced herself that her mother wished that she'd been a boy. "Only when you have the hair dryer going," her mother insisted.

Even though she's almost through her teen years, Jocelyn still feels so overwhelmed by having to raise her younger brother that she's decided never to have any kids of her own. She feels she's already had her child. She did it and, as she jokes, she kept her shape. No, she will not change her mind. When her father asked would it be all right with her if he got remarried, she said, okay

—under one condition. He and his new wife had better promise they would never have children. If they did, she would not be his daughter anymore.

Armando

A sixteen-year-old named Armando says he was a "confused little kid." He'd be withdrawn until one person would set him off and he'd explode. His first memory is of a fight between his mother and the man he now calls "his real dad." His father did drugs, and when his mother found him with heroin and a needle, she smashed the syringe on the sidewalk. Armando was three.

Until his mother finally threw his father out for the last time a few years later, he would appear and disappear, leaving behind broken promises and broken furniture. Armando has no idea where his father is today. He doesn't even know if he's alive. All he does know is that he has a hard time trusting people. At times he feels he's lived part of his life behind a wall, afraid to let others in or himself out.

Now he's in a funny position. His mother has remarried and he has two stepbrothers close in age. The three boys are often competitive about the girls they date. If Armando likes a particular girl, one or both of his stepbrothers seem to decide they do, too. After being an only child for most of his life, suddenly Armando is somebody's brother. The confused little kid has become a "confused older kid."

3

BOILING OVER

*"My grandmother—my father's mother—once
took a picture of my dad, my mom, my sister, my
dog Clarence—he was a dachshund—and myself. It was a very old picture and I was little.
My sister, Shallie, was little. It was our favorite
picture," says Kimberly, a seventeen-year-old
who currently lives in Houston, Texas.*

*"One day my sister moved out from my aunt's
where we'd been living because she and my aunt
got in a big fight. For years my sister and I
fought all the time. Anyway, I'd been out playing soccer with the guys. Afterwards, when I
went up to my room, I saw written in lipstick on
the mirror, 'Kimberly, I'm your big sister. I'll
always love you. Stay tight and I'll always be
there. Love, Shallie.'*

"That's the first time my sister ever said,

'Hey, I'm your big sister. I'll be there.' It brought tears to my eyes and I'm not a person to cry. I don't let things get to me. When I saw that, wow! *Real dark red lipstick written on the mirror.*

"And there on my dresser was that old family picture. I was so mad I just ripped out each person. I ripped out my mom. I ripped out my dad. I ripped out my sister. And my dog Clarence was out 'cause he'd died. I was the only one left in the picture. It made sense.

"I stayed in my room for the rest of the day. My mom came up and she saw the picture torn apart and she said, 'What is this saying?'

"I said, 'What do you mean, what is it saying? It's saying that we're not a family anymore.'

"She said, 'You and me are together.'

" 'When are you going to leave,' I said, because she left two times before. 'You'll leave again.' "

"In the beginning, there were the four of us. That lasted until I was about ten, when my parents separated. I was twelve when my parents really divorced.

"When we were little, me and my sister Shallie shared the same room. We had single beds. We would jump from one bed to the other. Then my dad would come in: 'Get to bed, kids.'

"My sister would come in bed with me and she would say, 'Kimberly, tell me a story.' I would tell her the stupidest stories that didn't make any kind of sense, but she'd still laugh because I said it. It was really cute. That memory, I'll take to my grave. After that, I have very

27

Before you can solve any sibling problems, you have to figure out the root causes. To start with, let's look at the simple fact that you're now a teenager, a potentially difficult period in many people's lives.

In their book *The Sibling Bond,* Michael D. Kahn and his coauthor write that life comes in a series of stages. As you grow and mature, sibling relationships change tremendously. Pretend, for example, that you are one of two children with just a couple of years separating you. That would mean in general from about the ages of three to five, you think about the world and spend your time in similar ways. And although from six to nine you may begin to have some different experiences, these are usually the easiest years together.[1]

During this early period, it's not unusual for you to share much of your life. You go back and forth to school together, confiding in each other about teachers and friends. After school and in the evenings, you probably play together.

By the time you turn ten, eleven, and twelve, you start to drift apart. You begin to become secretive. Your sense of being somehow different from your sisters and brothers increases. As you enter early adolescence, about thirteen and fourteen, your feelings of separateness grow powerful.[2] You are knee-deep in adolescence, the emotional roller coaster of life's stages. One minute you can feel absolutely confident, and ten minutes later you're insecure, convinced you're a jerk.

What psychiatrists and psychologists say is this: It's normal for you to want to end your former dependent,

28

little-kid stage. It's normal to want to have your parents and the rest of the world accept you as the adult and responsible person you feel you are. At this age, independence is your main goal.

In this struggle, however, many of you feel under siege and unable to cope. You lash out. You make the closest family members the targets of your inflamed emotions, discovering that you have the power to help or to hurt them. Some of you grow skilled at the vicious, verbal attack. You zero in on your siblings' most vulnerable areas—their achievements, sexuality, and looks. And as some of you know firsthand, a war of words can escalate into physical violence.

Others of you are the targets yourselves. A brother or sister leading a "life on the edge" makes your own life miserable. You're the one who winds up feeling you've been turned into a punching bag. Belittled, badgered, and continually assaulted, you wonder, Am I dying inside? To survive, you switch your emotions to "off."

When Jocelyn was twelve and her brother, Jason, was four, her mother had to go back to work. "From then on," says Jocelyn, who is now eighteen, "I practically raised him by myself. After a while, I got really upset about it. I can't believe it, I'd think. I make him dinner. I feed him. I dress him. I undress him. I give him a bath. I put him to bed.

"I'd been this very happy child, maybe a little spoiled. I never cried; that's what my mother always told me. All of a sudden, though, my father left and my mother couldn't work and handle Jason, too. I started to feel like Jason's mother, not his sister. There were even times

29

when he called me Mom, I was scared watching him and I figured, that's not right. He's just a baby. He should have his mom around.

"I'd get angry at him because he didn't pick up. And I got yelled at. Me. I was in school all day, and when I came home, I didn't want to have to pick up after him. Phooey! *I finally refused to go in and pick up his hundred cups and cereal bowls and stuff. I hated it.*

*"I'd tell him, '*I'm not your slave.*' But he didn't listen to me. I'd say, 'Jason, don't do that.* Jason, come back here!*' He'd just keep on walking.*

"To make this even worse, having to baby-sit all the time was ruining *my social life. This isn't going to sound very modest, but from the seventh grade until now, my senior year, I was notable. My group was the jocks, the popularity crowd. I've always had lots of friends. Anyway, on Friday night, I couldn't go anyplace because my mother was at work. In the beginning, it didn't matter as much since we didn't really have anywhere to go. We didn't know about keg parties yet. If we were into petting, we went to the movies and one of the mothers had to drive us.*

"Then I started to have boys over. Of course, I didn't tell my mother about it. When she found out, she got upset and said, 'I don't want any boys over!'

" 'Why? Do you think I'm going to run a motel! We sit around and watch a movie or something like that. If I'm not allowed to have some of my friends over, then I'm not baby-sitting anymore. It's *not fair* to me.'

30

> *"She said, 'This is hard for me, too.'*
> *"I said, 'Ma, I'm sure you could find a job*
> *with no night work.'*
> *"She said, 'Well, what are the boys' names?'*
> " 'Ma, I'm not a kid; I'm a teenager.' "

This Is Your Life

Whatever your own circumstances may be, in order to work on a sibling truce and an eventual peace treaty, you have to try to understand *yourself* better. You've got to look inside yourself and try to figure out, at this stage in your life, who you really are.

The experts say if they were helping you confront your own emotional strengths and weaknesses, they'd ask these kinds of questions:

- What would you say is important to you?
- How comfortable are you with who you are and what you look like?
- Can you pinpoint specific issues that you know are causing you problems, such as drugs or sex?
- How are you doing in school?
- Are you cutting class? Just getting by? Flunking out? On the verge of quitting?
- How would you ideally like to spend your time?
- Do you have close friends?
- Have friends replaced your family when it comes to emotional support? How do you feel about that?
- Do you feel out of control with no place to turn to regain stability?
- What words best describe how you feel inside?

31

If a self-evaluation tells you that when it comes to self-esteem, you're running on empty, the experts agree: The shakier you feel about yourself, the less you like yourself, the greater probability you'll have serious problems dealing with any sister or brother. [See Chapter 8 for ways to improve your self-esteem.]

What the experts also say is that to understand yourself and your sibling relations, you have to figure out how well something they call the "family system" or the "family script" is working.

4

THE PLAY'S THE THING

Getting along with sisters and brothers has always been tricky. But how come? Why is there so much tension? The answer is you don't operate on your own. Instead, you're a member of what therapists call a "family system" or a "family script." And lately more and more of these scripts seem to be haunted by problems. There could be a mother who works too hard, a sister who drinks all night, a father who doesn't care, and on and on.

Think of the family system as a play, says psychologist Dan Gottfried. In the script for this play, every family member is cast in a specific role. At the same time, each of you depends on the others to perform their roles, too. In order to have a successful play—for the family system to run smoothly—all the "actors" have to perform their parts. They have to stick to the script. It has to do with balance, says Gottfried.

Let's say, though, that one of the actors, an older

brother, always comes home loaded. He's loud and mean, antagonizing the rest of the cast members. One night he never even appears—no phone call, nothing. Two nights later he's back, but with no explanation. He shuts down and refuses to talk to anybody.

Although one or two of the other actors try to cover for him, it doesn't work. They're confused and angry. How could an important actor in their stage family let them down? They argue among themselves. "Why did this happen?" "It's your fault." "Not me. You're the one who's always on his case." One member tries to take over the older brother's role, as well as his own, something that's almost impossible. In the end, it's not surprising that they all feel lousy and the play falls apart.

For each of you, the family system—the family script —is like that play. Your behavior is affected by all the events and changes that happen to each member of your family and by the sum of how each plays his or her part. When one sibling is causing another one pain, you have to ask yourself: What exactly is going on in your family play?

5

READING THE SCRIPT

Today's family comes in all sizes and arrangements. The most common variety has one or two adults in charge and then there are the children—that's you and any sisters and brothers. Ideally, there is something therapists call a sibling bond among the kids. You and your siblings feel united and emotionally secure with each other. At the same time, there is a parental bond. Between these two different bonds is a clear division, a boundary. Kids are allowed to be kids. A parent or parents are the ones who run things and make the major decisions.

In some families, though, the barrier between the two bonds doesn't exist. Maybe your parents were teen parents themselves with little adult experience. Or maybe that barrier was once there, but has been eaten away by drugs, loss of employment, or other kinds of stress. Consequently, you barge in and out of your parent's personal life, no matter what he or she is doing. And the parent intrudes in your life with no sense of distance, either.

The parent is too involved in your activities, for example, demanding to hear every last detail of what you did on that date last night. There is not enough separateness between the child and the adult.

In some families, members are so enmeshed with one another that they don't have much of a social life beyond the family unit. The experts agree that this situation can bring on hostility, hate, and competition between brothers and sisters.

Fighting the Wrong War

Even when the separate sibling and parental bonds are in place, how your parents get along with each other influences how you get along with your sisters and brothers. Says therapist Margaret Hayner, some parents confuse you. They can't agree. Mom tells you one thing and Dad tells you something different. Problems are also created by parents who keep secrets from each other, who scream a lot, or who are depressed. Compulsive shopping, gambling, alcoholism, and spouse battering are other problems that lead to tension and trauma between your parents. This can then get fought out through their children.

What happens is this: You and your sibling fight more often when your parents aren't getting along. You fight after they fight; and when you fight, there's *less* tension between your mother and father. They seem to come together. Why? Because they have to stop to take care of your fighting; so to distract them from *their* anger, you fight some more.

What happens, too, is that there's a war going on and people take sides. You side with one parent against the other. You also fight with a sister or brother on your favorite parent's behalf. You get upset at the sibling whom you see being negative to that parent. You forget, this isn't your war; you're simply caught in their crossfire. The parent and the other sibling—not you—are responsible for dealing with their differences.

Parents play favorites, too. In some families, you're favored for your unique characteristics. In other families, the favoritism is extreme. One sibling receives unending praise, while another is always put down. The result here, too, is rivalry and anger between the kids involved.

Parents—Missing in Action

Some families, especially larger ones, wind up with what is known as a parental subsystem, a play within a play. If the parents give up control, maybe just because the family is big or because of outside job pressure, the kids become their stand-ins. But the younger siblings often resent being raised by a substitute mother and father, and having the power passed down to one of their own siblings. At the same time, the older siblings, usually the ones doing the parenting, can be overwhelmed. They don't have the maturity to parent. This family script spells trouble, too.

Even with two working parents, supporting today's family is a difficult juggling act. One or both of them may have travel schedules that keep them away for days at a time. They may work overtime, weekends, holidays, night shifts. When they're home, they're exhausted, distracted, or trying to escape. In your parents' drive to succeed, you might feel you and your siblings have been forgotten. To get their attention, you may fight.

All these problems can be part of the scripts of intact

37

families. When you add the changes and pressures brought on by divorce, poverty, or remarriage, the difficulties can increase dramatically.

About two years ago, when Cherisse, Darnell, and LaToya's mother was "troubled," she first sent her three children to live with one of their aunts. "We stayed with her and her three kids for six months," says Cherisse. "But finally, she had her own problems. Her husband, well, you could say he liked to use physical force.

"Another aunt, my mother's sister, Mary, took us in next, and each day Darnell was becoming a bigger pain than the day before. He was so bad, I even got a beating 'cause of him. Okay, Aunt Mary was making up the beds and found some cigarettes under mine. I walk in from school and Aunt Mary says, 'Cherisse, come into the kitchen and, Darnell, you, too. Whose cigarettes are these?'

"I say, 'They're not mine.' But I know Darnell put them under my bed. I'm trying to protect him.

"So Darnell says, 'They're not mine; they're Cherisse's.'

"I say, 'Hold up. I'm telling the truth! Don't story on me.' So I told my aunt and I got a beating, because I covered up and lied in my aunt's face. Darnell got a beating, too, but I really got a beating because I was older, should have known better, and all that.

"I asked Darnell how come he lied, but he didn't have an answer. Since nobody seems to

> *care about him, it's like he doesn't care either.*
> *He just does things."*

The Exploding Family

Half the marriages in America end in divorce.[1] And
when one explodes in the center of a family, all the
members are changed and wounded. You might be so
thrown emotionally that you feel out of order. (The same
holds true for a parent.) While you may be okay on the
outside, inside you're functioning on automatic pilot.
One teenager, pointing to her head, calls it the "nobody's
home" syndrome.

For some, the response to the first explosion is another. You deal with separation and divorce with action.
You slice off your hair, rearrange your life, and an-
nounce you are becoming a different person. Regardless
of how each individual reacts, one thing is clear. Nobody
escapes a divorce unscathed. In fact, separation and divorce come with a radically altered script.

("How come all of a sudden Mom's having you do all
the driving?" "Well, how come Dad's suddenly confiding
in you?" "Whaddaya mean, do this, do that? You can't
tell me what to do! You're not my parent." "Mom, why
are we eating with a bunch of strangers on Thanksgiv-
ing, anyway?")

Those left behind in a disintegrating marriage scram-
ble to regroup, to fill the gap of the now-missing lead
member. What you need is a new balance. What you
often want, though, is to get back what you lost. Even if
what you had as a family wasn't that hot, it was what
you had. It's different now, and you don't want it to be

different. The changes don't feel right. So you fight the change by fighting each other.

You cannot expect a family to be calm during such an upheaval. Parents feel guilty. You feel deprived. And for kids, unlike some adults, the fallout from divorce doesn't disappear within a couple of years. According to many experts, divorce issues resurface in your teen years. Psychologist Dr. Paul Coiteux says what he sees in his counseling is that your home life might have seemed smooth through your middle years—five to ten, eleven, or twelve. But by the time you enter your teens, the conflicts return. Very often that's when you recognize that you're still upset about the divorce that might have taken place even a decade ago. Those conflicts often turn into problems between siblings.

Growing Up Broke

More than half the poor families in America today are made up of single mothers and their children.[2] Some of you have been living this reality since birth. Some of you once had more comfortable years. Then because parents get laid off or divorced, or for other reasons, you find yourself growing up poor.

Your parent or parents may feel overwhelmed trying to stretch the family income. They could feel defeated. They may be so physically and emotionally burned, that although they wish they could, they can't fill their assigned role in the family script. You yourself could feel the same way.

Without money to cover the bills, you're walking a high wire with no safety net. Will the roof over your head be there tonight? Will you have to double-up and triple-up with cousins, grandmothers, neighbors? Your family script could even include life on the streets or in a shelter. (Every fourth homeless person is a child.)[3] There may be days when the only things left to eat in your home are mayo and ketchup. New clothes have to be a low priority in the family budget. When it comes to money in your pocket, you're on your own.

One out of five of you—20 percent—is coming of age in poverty.[4] If you're African American, the figure is far grimmer: nearly half of you under the age of eighteen are living in poverty.[5] Experts have learned that this extracts a huge emotional toll, resulting in serious mental and emotional problems. Few who are enduring this fate receive help.[6]

Then add this factor. Your community also plays a part in your script. It helps mold and shape how you deal with your other family members. With limited income for a place to call home, you might find yourself in a neighborhood that's dangerous: turf wars, drug wars, drive-by shootings. Gangs confront you when you step out the door. There are kids around bent on terrorizing you. Free time, stress, and self-preservation may conspire to lead you, a sibling, or a parent to cross the line into drugs and crime.

There is so much violence in many of your lives, that the most you can wish for is that those around you will not use weapons. You hope they'll fight it out with their fists. As you hear about the latest teenager to die, it's not a far leap to imagine one sibling—particularly a male— killing another.

"I'd really wanted a brother or sister since I was God knows how old. When it happened for real, though, it all happened so quick. I was used to it being just me and my mom, and one morning, she got remarried. Then it was me

> *and my mom and my dad-now and Xavier and Desmond and then Michael, the baby," says sixteen-year-old Armando.*
>
> *"At first I was excited to have brothers, especially a baby, in the house. But then I saw all the attention he was getting. I didn't like it. I was used to all the attention being given to me. One day my mother said, 'Watch the baby.'*
>
> *"Without really thinking, I picked up the pillow and put it over his face. I tried to smother Michael. I didn't know that anything would happen. I thought the baby was like a toy."*

The New and Improved Family

Every day an average of 1,300 new stepfamilies are formed.[7] Experts call them remarried families, blended families, reconstituted families, even accordion families, expanding and contracting with his kids and hers.

("It's the second Saturday in the month, so you're due at your father's. Clean up your room before you go. Your stepsisters will be using it." "But, *Maaaa . . .*")

Whatever name you use, it's predicted that by the year 2000, this will be the most common family combination in the land.[8] Being a member of a remarried family is a challenge. It's a ready-made stage on which sibling battles can and do play out. If you're older and you suddenly have to start living with stepsiblings, the tension is intense.

For starters, a remarried family is a much more sexual place than a biological family, says psychiatrist Dr. John Visher. You're with an adult couple—your parent and a new partner—who are in the middle of a honeymoon. They're showing much more physical affection and appreciation of each other than most "real" parents do. Or, at least, you're particularly aware of this attraction. You can't convince yourself, says Dr. Visher, that these two adults don't have a sexual relationship, the way you do with your biological parents.

And overnight, you find that you have to share with kids who are different. (Each of you is convinced that how *you* celebrate New Year's Eve is the right way; and can you believe it, your stepsiblings don't tape the soap operas to watch after school?) Meanwhile, you're supposed to feel close to this stranger—a stepsibling—whom you didn't even choose.

With everything out of balance, life becomes a series of adjustments and negotiations. Some members are working on a new family script, while others are still plotting the return of the old one. For some of you, too, this isn't the first time or possibly the last time that one of your parents has tried to live happily ever after. Now you practically need a chart to keep everyone straight. And no one—not you, your parent, stepparent, your own siblings, or any stepsiblings—is sure about his or her role.

It's a shock. One day your mom's the boss and the next day along comes this replacement. Or you were getting all the benefits of being the oldest, and the next day, those privileges vanish. You probably were comfortable with your role in your former family, says psychologist Dr. Emily Visher. You didn't even think about it. Then out of the blue, it's all gone. You have new brothers and sisters.

These new siblings may be your age; they may be older. They may be cute babies who sleep all the time. If they are babies who are now the center of attention, you may feel that your importance is even further diminished. According to Dr. John Visher, Dr. Emily Visher, and the other experts queried, no one should be surprised if these dramatic changes cause problems for everyone.

6

FIRST-BORN,
SECOND-BORN . . .

Until her eleventh birthday, Essence was an oldest child
with a younger half sister, Alexandria, being raised by
their single mother. At the same time, though, Essence's
father had several children from earlier relationships.
In this man's life, Essence was his youngest, his "baby."
Then Alexandria was killed in a hit-and-run accident.
For the next year, in her mother's eyes, Essence was an
only child. To fill the void created by the child's death,
Essence's mother decided to open her doors to foster children. At last count there have been thirteen. Meanwhile, when Essence turned fifteen, her mother married
a man with two children, one the same age as Essence
and the other younger. When asked where she falls in
her family birth order, Essence replies, "You tell me."

Does Birth Order Matter?

The experts are divided on the role birth order plays. Some believe that birth order plays a critical role in how you get along with your siblings—and in life.[1] Check a room full of oldest children, they say, and you discover that those who are first-born share certain personality characteristics, including certain ways they interact with brothers and sisters. The same holds true for a room full of middle children, as well as for the youngest.

The same experts also believe that except for oldest and only children, these characteristics develop as you try to cope with the next older child. For example, the second-born has to deal with the overachieving first-born. The third-born must cope with the perfectionist second-born. The fourth-born has to contend with the strong-willed third-born. (According to this theory, in large families, the birth-order characteristics repeat with the fifth, ninth, thirteenth, and seventeenth child.)

What About Parents' Birth Order?

Parents' birth order can be a factor in behavior, too. First-born parents want respect, not love, and they use punishment to get it. They like to compare the behavior of their children and may have the biggest conflicts with their third-born child.

Because second-born parents strive for perfection, they don't feel adequate to the job. They are often hardest on the oldest and easiest on the second-born.

Third-born parents can be the kindest, most understanding, and patient. They don't let things bother them the way other parents do.

Because fourth-born parents may not have had any experience caring for siblings, they may have a tough time parenting. Psychologically, they aren't prepared for it.

Only-child parents don't know how siblings are supposed to get along. Instead, they may depend on their spouse or partner to do most of the parenting.

Me First!

Other experts disagree with the importance of birth order.[2] Birth order is important, they say, but no more than a lot of factors. You have to consider such issues as whether the child is male or female, how many kids there are in the family, the number of years between them, and even the particular race and culture.

Looking at birth order alone, you find problems. Take the middle child. A person sandwiched between siblings a year younger and a year older is different from someone who's in the middle of siblings eight years younger and older. The closer you are in age, the more intense your relationship is likely to be. Two siblings separated by more than six years begin to act more like only children, singletons. To further complicate matters, the middle position can cover a lot of territory. You might be the middle of three kids or ten, not a small difference.

There are, however, truths about birth order. Whether you're related by birth or marriage, older siblings are usually bigger than the younger ones. And bigger means privilege—me first!—and power—I'll get you! Aside from that, in these experts' opinions, what number child you are in your family script influences maybe 10 to 20 percent of your behavior and how you deal with each other.

Think of birth order like astrology. There are many believers, but there is no solid proof of its value. After reading the profiles below, *you* decide how accurate these descriptions are. Can you find yourself? If so, use this information to help you clarify your own situation. If they're off base, skip ahead to the next chapter.

"We're really different," says Kimberly, talking about her sister, Shallie, who's now nineteen. *"My sister is a Miss Priss type. She's the first born, of course, and Grandmom's favorite. I have a bad attitude, they say. I'm more like my father, more outgoing, more athletic.*

"Shallie is just like my mom. It makes me sick. My mom is really dependent on others. She can't do anything for herself, which is sad. Sometimes she'll borrow money from me for no reason at all or because she doesn't want to work. At times, I feel like I have to give it to her because of everything she did for me when I was little. I sometimes wonder if I had more brothers and sisters if I would have done the things I did when I was little.

"I was never spoiled, though. The only person who ever said I was was my sister. But I was hyperactive. My mom was going to put me on Ritalin. My dad said no. That was right around when I was ten, and they were in the process of separating. My parents argued about it. They argued about lots of things. My dad has a short temper. I think I inherited it.

"Shallie and I always argued, too. We fought so many times, I don't remember what about. Probably 'cause of boys. She always had that look. All the guys in the neighborhood knew. Being twelve and thirteen years old at the time,

*she was maturing fast. She was the prettiest
girl around. I had thick glasses and pigtails.*

*"When she called me the Ugly Duckling one
too many times, I picked up this thirty-five-
pound pottery fruit bowl. It was old and be-
longed to my grandmother. I threw it at Shallie
and hit her head. She was out cold for quite
some hours. I didn't know what to do. My mom
and dad were both out working. It was like—
well, here you see this poor kid who was so
scared. I was about ten. I freaked out. I left.*

*"We lived in apartments then, and I just ran
around the apartments crying. When my mom
came home, she called the hospital. The ambu-
lance came and my dad was so mad at me. I
was more punished by hurting his feelings than
anything. I was the kid who would go with my
dad to the store that was two minutes down the
road just to be sitting next to him. To know that
I really hurt him was the worst thing that
could ever happen to me."*

Leaders or Lazy?

First-born. If you're the oldest, your parent learned
how to parent on you. You're the first to experience everything, including discipline. You're disciplined more
harshly than any children who come later. Still, you do
start out in the spotlight, a parent's dream for the future. That means pressure on you to succeed, and first-
borns do seem to end up more often in leadership positions.

The words used to describe you are *well organized,*

*listmaker, reliable, conscientious, serious, scholarly, con-
servative,* and *traditional.*

First-borns grow up wanting approval, admiration,
and respect. In the process, though, you sometimes lose
track of what *you* want, need, and feel. Under certain
circumstances, you can be a real problem. You demand
obedience from those you feel are inferior to you. You're
bossy. You can also be obnoxious, lazy, lawless, and violent—if that's what impresses those with whom you as-
sociate.

What you have to cope with in terms of birth order is
the loss of the attention you've gotten when the second-
born arrives. Although you've been told this baby is going to be fun, in your opinion, it's not true. While adjusting to this new arrival, you learn you receive more
praise for doing good than grumbling. It is this that
drives you for much of your life.

Inadequate Perfectionist?

Second-born. If you're the second-born, from day one,
whenever you do something, the first-born tries to out-
perform you. You feel inadequate. To make up for that,
you become a realistic perfectionist: because you can't be
perfect at everything, you select one area in which to
achieve. The result could be that while your room is a
mess, your homework is perfect. Second-born teenagers
have been known to practice posture movements and fa-
cial expressions in front of a mirror.

When the second-born is also a middle child, you have
the freedom to go about your business without anybody
paying much attention to you. Some experts feel that
middle children have the best position. You have an
older sibling to rely on, and you are the competent one in

relation to those who follow you. You avoid conflict and have many friends to whom you're extremely loyal.

The down side is that you're picked on by the older ones and get into trouble for picking on the younger ones. The larger the family, the harder the middle role is. Then there are always many older children who are more capable than you, and many younger children competing for attention. You also have the fewest pictures in the family photo album.

Charming Troublemaker?

Third-born. If you're the third-born, you arrive into an already-complicated family script of who's getting along with whom and who isn't. Once you figure it out, you don't take sides. How you feel about yourself is very connected to the stability of your parents' relationship. You move slowly and cautiously and you need to know you're appreciated.

The challenge for you is to defend against the second-born, who tries to pass on to you his or her own feelings of inadequacy. The second-born makes fun of you and insists that you can't do anything right. Your parent tells you to ignore it. When you follow that advice, you turn off your feelings. You convince yourself you are fearless and strong. The catch is that adults say that your sense of fearlessness makes you difficult to control. A large percentage of teenagers who get in trouble are third-born.

You also like to show off and blame others. However, you're a charming people-person, engaging and precocious. You care deeply about the weak and helpless with whom you identify. You seek nonthreatening relationships and use humor to keep an emotional distance from others.

51

Loving Brat?

Fourth-born. While the first-born pays attention to details, the fourth-born looks at the big picture. When you were a baby, your parents tried to decide how to keep the family script running smoothly. As you grow up, your role became to help in this job. You're the trouble-shooter, signaling when and where there's a breakdown. You see pain in a family member and try to make it better. Because you're highly demonstrative, you're good at interacting with others.

The third-born has the greatest impact on you. He or she tries to make you feel vulnerable. Instead, you feel immature. You constantly hear that you're not old enough, big enough, or fast enough to play with the older siblings. You feel excluded, frustrated. None of them will listen to you. To get their attention, you may resort to hitting.

If you're also the youngest, you're babied by everyone. That's probably why you're accused of being self-centered. You get attention, but not very much credit. Because you're the newest and smallest member of the family, you don't have much power. It's hard for the baby to be in charge of anything. You may find that you get more than your share of blame for all sorts of things, and lots of misinformation from your older siblings. It's also been said that you never stop talking. Maybe you're busy passing on all that misinformation.

What do you think?

7

PRESSURE POINTS

When teenagers tell school psychologist Dr. Coiteux that their siblings are making them crazy, he shows them a kind of stress test.[1] This is a series of statements about possible pressure points—events and changes—that may have been occurring in their lives, especially in the last twelve months. As they go over the list together, Dr. Coiteux asks, what's going on in your household? On top of any long-term difficulties, have there been a lot of changes in your family script lately?

Change sets off a falling-domino reaction. *Any* life change, good or bad, increases the pressure on you. This pressure, in turn, affects your body and your mind. A lot of change and pressure, particularly in a short period of time, can literally make you sick. You may have more colds, headaches, and even ulcers. Emotionally, you may become sad and withdrawn, or aggressive and loud. A lot of change can even cause what psychologist Dr. Neil Bernstein calls depressive equivalents: drug overdoses, sexual promiscuity, and risk-taking behavior such as driving too fast and joining fringe groups or gangs.

Any life change that touches one family member touches all members. For example, if a parent loses a job, everybody in the family suffers. Every member worries. The pressure on the whole family rises. And what do you do to release that anxiety? You very often take it out on each other.

Below is a list of pressure points compiled from interviews with experts and teens, and patterned after the test used by Dr. Coiteux, as well as other psychologists nationwide. Read through the entries. Did any of these types of events and changes take place in your life, especially in the last year? Although many of these events may be beyond your control, they could well result in sibling conflict.

PRESSURE POINT LIST

- A parent or sibling died.
- You became a parent.
- Your parents separated or divorced.
- There is verbal, physical, or sexual abuse in your home.
- You or a member of your immediate family (parents or sibling) is an alcoholic, drug abuser, chronic gambler, or has been institutionalized.
- You or a member of your family was arrested or served time in jail.
- You live with a parent and a stepparent.
- You live with at least one stepsibling, too.
- You live in a group home or with a foster family.
- You live in a high-crime neighborhood.
- A new sibling was born.

- You became pregnant (female) or contributed to a pregnancy (male).
- You placed a child in adoption or foster care.
- You had an abortion.
- You had a miscarriage.
- You were the victim of a violent crime.
- You or a member of your family was badly injured or had a serious illness.
- You are an immigrant or refugee.
- A parent was fired from a job.
- You changed schools.
- You were suspended from school.
- You took the S.A.T.
- You experienced extensive pressure to achieve.
- You broke up with your boyfriend/girlfriend.
- You were fired from a job.
- You or a member of your immediate family earned money illegally.
- A close friend of yours died.
- You or a parent started a new job.
- You worked part-time more than fifteen hours a week.
- You moved.

8

TAKING CHARGE OF YOURSELF

"I'm a middle kid," says Anne-Marie, sixteen
years old. *"My brother was seven when I was
born. He used to tell me he wanted to name me
Lollipop. He'd teach me stuff, like how to follow
the dots. It made him feel important and it
made me feel good.*

*"When I was four or five, though, my mom got
really busy working. She made my brother my
baby-sitter. He'd say, let's make a pact: we never
tell on each other. At first I said, sure. But then,
well, he began to pester me. He was always tick-
ling me and making me squirm. It didn't seem
funny to me.*

*"He'd come into the bathroom when I was in
the tub and say, I'll wash the front and you
wash the back. Finally, it got worse. I guess I
was about seven when he raped me. My mother*

found out because I started having trouble uri-
nating. And you know what she said? She was
just like the mother in the book Pride and Prej-
udice *that we've been reading in English class.*
She said, 'Ohhh, this is so upsetting to me. You
have to make up, because I can't take it.' Not,
what could she do to help me. Not, she's throw-
ing my brother out. Just 'make up and forget it.
God will protect you.'

"I went to confession and told the priest. He
said, 'Your mother was right; forget it.' Then
Sunday in his sermon he talked about a girl in
the parish that had been raped by her brother.
The priest didn't say my name, but I was there.
I thought I was going to die. I felt he betrayed
me. He shouldn't have told what I said in con-
fession. I stopped going to mass.

"Later my brother said, can we make up?
Make up! I don't think he understood. My
mother thought I was being irrational. She told
me to drop it. She wouldn't deal with it. But
then he started to pester my little sister. That
was it. Finally, my mother said he had to move
out of the house. Now he's married and has his
own child. I worry, what kind of father must
he be?"

In Chapter 3, the experts said that the less you like yourself, the more sibling problems you'll have. They all
emphasize that what is crucial to improving these relationships is first to work on yourself. Improve *your* self-
esteem. This chapter is devoted to techniques aimed at

helping you do just that. If you've decided to try, here's a plan.

Make yourself your own project. And as with any major project, break this one down into small, manageable pieces. This is called "control mastery." It helps you develop confidence and a feeling that you can handle old *and* new situations.

Skim the eight tasks below. Then pick, say, two of them that seem the most interesting to you or the most within your reach. You're the problem solver. No one else can tell you exactly what to do because the best plans come from your own head. Be flexible. Tailor the task to fit your needs. (Tackling them all at once is too much to expect of yourself.)

You must also stick with trying to improve these particular areas of your life for a minimum of the next *six* months. That may seem like forever, but the problems you're having didn't happen in a single night either. In the end, you *will* feel and see the difference. You'll be happier, more motivated, and in control. Your self-image will improve dramatically. Then if you like yourself better, you may discover that sibling troubles seem more easily resolved, too.

BASICS

---

1. *Life Patterning.* Develop a daily routine, a schedule. This is the foundation upon which you can design your new life. To start with, pick an appropriate hour and see if you can wake up Monday through Friday at about that same time. Make it early enough so that you can get to school with everything you need. You might want to ease your morning rush by organizing what you need the night before.

58

Once at school, tell yourself you're going to make it to each class on time. After school, too, maintain some kind of routine. Whatever you do —work, play a sport, or go right home—block out that period of time as well. Then plan your evenings. Pick a specific time when you do each thing you want to accomplish: help around the house, study, telephone, keep a journal, watch TV. Then find a realistic hour to go to bed and wake up the next day to begin again.

To help you achieve this life patterning, refine it and come up with a few rituals. Take a series of activities and do them exactly the same each time. (First, wash your hands, sharpen a pencil, get out some paper, open your school book, turn off the TV, and then start that homework.) Rituals help keep your mind off outside pressures, focus your attention on the here and now, and create situations where you can become totally absorbed in what you're doing. This goal is to reach a point where you forget about everything except the task at hand.

2. *Work Out.* Do whatever it takes to get your body moving. For example, don't use the elevator. Walk. For variety, try running up the stairs. If you live in an apartment on a high floor, every other time don't ride. At a local gym, run, walk, skip, jump rope, bike, swim, do gymnastics or aerobics. Play handball, volleyball, basketball, ping-pong.

Dance. Skateboard. Surf. Ride. When you're staring at the TV, do leg lifts. Clean house with enough energy to work up a sweat. And do these physical activities on a schedule and at least three times a week.

59

3. *Food Fight.* Today, television ads, and even your family bombard you with messages about the perfect body shape. Females hear, you're too fat and fat is ugly. Males, you're told that big muscles are heroic. Without them, you're a nerd, a wimp. The result is that starting at younger and younger ages, you learn to hate your body. To try to change your shape, many of you begin compulsive eating—fad diets, starving, and binging. *Stop.*

Your body is an amazing mechanism, which, given half a chance, will tell you when and what to eat. Your job is to listen. In other words, at first let body hunger be the guide, and your body will tell you when it's time for food. Don't be concerned about limiting your choices; don't judge yourself. Simply eat. You want to learn to eat without compulsion and dieting. In fact, starving yourself is the major cause of out-of-control eating. And the food you binge on is the same food you spend the rest of your time trying to avoid.

When you eat, you're trying to soothe yourself in some way. Try to figure out what emotions you might be dealing with. For example, sugar is strong competition for anxiety. When reaching for that cookie, what are you really reaching for? What's not okay in your life? You're looking for the feelings, the emotional hunger that is often confused with body hunger. When eating without fear, you'll eventually achieve what is your own natural body weight. Maybe it's not the model-perfect image, but you're the one who's living in your skin and you'll be happier.

Once you relax about what you eat, start making food choices based on what's best to lead a longer, healthier life. There are books about nutrition in your library. Check them out. For the time being, though, here are a few suggestions on how to proceed.

In general, unless you have restrictions against it, eat a variety of fruits and vegetables, whole grains, beans, lean meats, chicken, and fish. Drink low-fat milk and plenty of water. When stopping by the store, instead of buying a candy bar, reach for an orange, a papaya, a melon. Pick up juice, not soda. If you're at a fast-food place, to reduce how much fat you eat, ask them to hold the mayo and other sauces. Eat pizza without the cheese. Take the breading off fried foods. If you just must have red meat, go for a roast beef sandwich rather than a hamburger. Better yet, try rice and beans. Make salads part of your diet. And while you're at it, season your food with lemon, not salt.

Here's a list compiled by Dr. Michael Jacobson's consumer advocacy group of the ten worst fast-food meals from the standpoint of their overall (lack of) nutritional value. For health and fun, see how long you can go without eating one of these: Wendy's Triple Cheeseburger, Burger King Double Beef Whopper with Cheese, Burger King Double Beef Whopper, Dairy Queen Triple Hamburger with Cheese, Carl's Jr. Super Star Hamburger, Jack in the Box Supreme Nachos, Jack in the Box Bacon Cheeseburger Supreme, Burger King Specialty Chicken Sandwich, Jack in the Box Swiss & Bacon Burger, and Roy Rogers RR Bar Burger.

4. *A Star Is Born*. Cultivate a talent, a skill, a specialized knowledge, a hobby—something you like

to do. Maybe you're the class clown. Or you're good at makeup, cutting hair, coming up with dramatic outfits. You have a great voice. You collect comic books, matches, salamanders, weird pieces of glass. You can speak more than one language. You know all about cars. You're solid in math, gym, communications, typing, whatever.

Select a particular skill; no one else can do it for you. Then give yourself some recognition, a pat on the back. You are someone special. Psychologist Ed Farrar says therapists call this "self-recognized competency." It's important, he says, for you to recognize that there are certain things you're good at, better than others around you. Then you must also recognize the opposite: sometimes you (and everybody else in the world) fail. Accept your weaknesses, too.

Now take your talent a step farther: use it to help others. If you're good in a subject, tutor a student in trouble. Are you a good listener? Get involved with or help start a peer counseling program at school. Is talking on the phone your favorite occupation? Volunteer to make calls for someone who can't manage, someone who doesn't speak much English or is hearing impaired. You're the local double-dutch champion (retired), a fine ballplayer, or a cook? Share this skill.

5. *Calm Down.* To reduce tension and anxiety, try a kind of meditation. Do the following three steps a couple of times a day for about five minutes. It's okay if you skip a day or two every now and then, but try not to miss doing this exercise when it's been a rotten day or you feel like exploding.

Step One: Find a private place. If your family

lives in one or two rooms, go into a corner and face the wall with your back to everyone around. Then sit or lie down, getting as comfortable as you can. You want to relax.

Step Two: Begin to take deep and even breaths. While doing this, try to concentrate on one thing. Some people like to focus on what they're doing. In their mind, they follow the flow of the air as it moves through the nose, down the throat, into the lungs, and back out again. Others like to focus on a particular number or a special word, sometimes called a mantra. Still others let their imaginations soar.

If you're a dreamer, picture a quiet place where you'd love to be. It can be made up or real. Start by thinking about how you get there, perhaps going down a staircase, one step at a time. Think about every detail: it's a weathered, wooden staircase leading to a peaceful beach.

Once there, choose a spot where you feel at ease and where you can come back to. Think of this as your power spot. If you're at the ocean, breath in rhythm with the waves coming in and going out. By the time some people have mentally brought themselves to this power spot, they've fallen asleep. It doesn't matter. The point of this exercise is to relax, let go of stress, and feel in control.

Step Three: While you're concentrating on this one thing, don't worry if you think about other things, too. Just keep refocusing on your breathing, a number, word, or image. Don't worry about how well you're doing. This is a time to forget.

For those of you who see a link between pressure and a specific health problem, Dr. Peter

Thomashow says check with a doctor about adding a fourth step: keeping a diary to chart events and symptoms. With help, you can break the pain-anxiety-pain cycle: your headache (pain) freaks you out (anxiety) and makes the headache worse (pain).

6. *Don't Live in the Endless Now.* Lots of you think that what your life is like now is the way it will be forever. You feel, what can I do? The sibling who's making me miserable will *always* be making me miserable. Or you feel you have reasons for being what some might consider a bully. You were standing up for your rights. In either case, you spend so much energy hating a sibling that you don't realize changes can be made.

People change. You can respond to each other. It can also be up to you whether you're willing to start the process. You could be the one who makes a difference. You could be the one who stops the fights instead of starts them, the one who goes for help instead fueling the flames.

Begin now to plan what you want your life to be like when you get out of the house. Come up with a mental picture of your future—and what you have to do to get there. If you want to go to college, you have to plan ahead, get involved with your classes, study, do homework, all that kind of stuff. You want to be a chef? Start now by trying to get a job at a restaurant. Tell the person who hires you about your goal and ask if there's anything he or she can do to help you. Computer programmer? Find out what you have to do at this point and then get started. Today.

7. *Reach Out.* Find out what clubs, youth groups or support programs there are in your school or

neighborhood that you could join that serve your needs. The choice is yours. Maybe you're interested in joining an acting group or a club devoted to a cause that's important to you, such as the environment. You could participate in a Big Brother or Big Sister program, a religious organization, Alcoholics Anonymous, Alateen, or Cocaine Anonymous—which leads us to number eight.

8. *Adopt an Adult.* Care about someone; connect emotionally with another human being. Find an adult you feel can be trusted to hear your thoughts. You need this person to offer you information, advice, and help; to remind you what a special individual you are. He or she needs you, as well, to keep up on the latest trends, to learn what's happening in your school, and to retain the perspective teenagers have on life.

Think of adults as teenagers with dry skin and wrinkles. They're human beings, too, and many of them actually have more wisdom than you might believe. They've experienced more of life's lessons. Even if you reach out to someone, and something happens that makes you feel betrayed, do it again. Life without caring is empty.

Maybe the adult is your parent. Maybe not. You can't always expect quality parenting, especially when the parent's a drug addict, an alcoholic, a spouse abuser, broke, underemployed, or not even there. But all adults are not alike. Look around. There are options: a teacher, a school counselor, a coach, the parent of a friend, an older neighbor, a friend of your parent, a grandfather, an aunt, an older cousin, a clergyman, a

director of a youth program, a nurse, a doctor.
Start talking to adults.

*"I try to remember what the lives of my foster
brothers and foster sisters were like when they
weren't living here with me," says sixteen-year-
old Essence. "But sometimes I just don't care
that Taylor had to eat dog food, or that Buddy's
parents would lock him in the car if he misbe-
haved. Go to another home, your own home, a
group home, I think to myself.*

*"The worst of it is the fighting—and over the
dumbest things, too. Like yesterday Taylor
started one with me. She was telling on me and
I told her not to. It wasn't true that I didn't
keep my bathroom clean. Then, as soon as that
was settled, there was a fight about who took
the pencil off the table. Next thing I knew my
mother got into it.*

"She said, 'Who'd steal a pencil?'

*"Everyone said stuff like, 'It wasn't me. Not
me.' How can you know, anyway, when there're
so many people?*

*" 'Moosehead did it,' Buddy finally said, us-
ing his name for Emily, Mom's favorite.*

*"My mom said, 'Shut up, Buddy. You have
Kermit-the-Frog eyes,' ending the fight by making him feel bad. That's her way.*

*"To get back at her, he broke up his room and
a brand new guitar she'd bought him. My mom
said, 'That's it.' She called up a social worker
and the social worker talked to other people
and finally Buddy was sent to another home.*

"There are times I wish I was a foster child or

66

adopted or a stepkid, too. Then when I get in a big fight with my mother, I could use that against her. I could say, 'You're not my natural mother. Leave me alone.' But she is, so I can't, so I just leave the room angry."

9

REWORKING THE FAMILY SCRIPT

In Chapter 8 you learned ways you could start solving sibling problems by working on yourself. Now let's look at the other pieces in your family puzzle. You can't cure your family problems without reworking the family script. Sit down and figure out what's going on at home with the other members. Remember the Pressure Point List in Chapter 7? What if one of your siblings or a parent reads the list? What changes have they been experiencing? How do these changes affect you and this war between you and your brother or sister?

Kimberly

In one year, Kimberly shared an apartment with two school friends. Then she moved back in with her mother, who was in a relationship with an angry alcoholic.

Kimberly's sister, Shallie, showed up after a breakup with her boyfriend.

Kimberly moved again, this time from Wisconsin to Texas to be with her father. He was adjusting to life in a mobile home with his latest woman-friend and her eleven-year-old. This move meant that Kimberly's senior year was in a school where everyone knew everyone else and she didn't know a soul. It also meant that her father was trying to please his new partner, get to know her daughter, and reacquaint himself with his own daughter, a person he hadn't seen much over the last few years.

Every member of Kimberly's extended family was caught in a tornado of emotions. They had all gone through so much during the year that none of them had a clear idea of what was expected of him or her or who he or she was supposed to be. And none could help the others.

Essence

Essence, who lives with foster, step-, and adopted siblings, in addition to her biological mother and new stepfather, scores high on any pressure-point list. With so many faces and personalities around, Essence is not even sure from one day to the next who makes up her family's cast of characters. All the new members who walk through the door bring with them both real and emotional baggage from their previous homes. Essence has a lead in "Fiorello," her school play, and feels that her mother doesn't care. She has no time for her own daughter.

In Essence's opinion, her mother's attention lately has focused on three of the foster children. One is fifteen and pregnant. The other two used a knife on each other to settle an argument over a belt.

Friends tell Essence, oh, your mother is doing such a good thing. She's providing love for all those children. Essence feels like answering, but she's *not* giving love. She's giving a house and getting money. Those are the things that are important to her. Meanwhile, Essence's mother feels trapped by her job of first cleaning other people's houses and then cleaning her own. Six months ago, she got married and she's giving her husband a little attention. She's sorry, she says, but she doesn't have time to deal with Essence's jealousy and sibling rivalry.

"Sometimes I wish we'd get rid of LaToya, the baby," says Darnell, who's now living with his sisters at their grandmother's. "It's always Toya, Toya, Toya around here. I scream at Toya, and then Cherisse screams at me for doing it, and pretty soon they're both screaming at me. That's what happens when you're in the middle.

"I see my mother over at her sister's every now and then. She says, 'If Cherisse tells you to do something, you do it.'

"We get back here and Cherisse puts a silly grin on her face and says, 'Darnell, you stop trying to boss Toya around. Darnell, don't put your hands on Toya. Darnell, you're not Toya's father.'

"But I never listen to Cherisse. Maybe I'm not Toya's father, but Cherisse's not my mother."

Cherisse has this to say: "When I see my mother, usually she lectures me. 'Cherisse,' she says, 'I'm not saying what you do is wrong or right, but before you do certain things, think about what it'll mean tomorrow.' But the thing is—how I do is how I feel? Like I found out my girlfriend is gay. Well, Darnell had to get in on it, too, saying in front of my mother, 'Cherisse, your friend is gay. How can you hang out with her?'

"My mother says, 'Cherisse, don't go around with her.' And I know she said that 'cause my friend is gay. But we've been friends a long time.

"I got so mad. 'We are close!' I tell her. 'If she's gay, she's gay! It's not her fault. It's not my fault. I'm not going to be gay.' Then my mother got angry at me for holding the wrong tone of voice toward her. Darnell's there listening, just hoping I'll get it; and the last thing I want to do is get my mother angry. I want to do things to make her happy. I miss her.

"Before I left that day, my mother told me, 'She can still be your friend, and I want you to know that I love you. I didn't mean to holler at you. I'm sorry.' Boy, was Darnell mad that I didn't get a beating."

Rivals, Rivalry: two or more striving to obtain something that only one can possess

According to the experts, when a family script is filled with changes and pressures, sibling problems are the frequent result. And one problem that seems to come up often is rivalry between sisters and brothers. It has to do with loss, says Dr. John Visher. When another family member arrives on the scene, whether the child is biological, adopted, step-, or foster, someone's losing. When another sibling starts taking up more of a parent's time, you feel your territory is shrinking. What attention you had has been taken away. Everyone has to adjust to the script changes.

It makes sense for you to feel angry and ignored when this happens, says therapist Joanne Althoff. You want Mom and Dad to be there for you and suddenly they're not. You've got to share not only their affection, but maybe your room. Sibling rivalry intensifies when everyone is living in close quarters and without much money. You don't have space for yourselves and you have to compete for the limited family resources.

Some of the experts say they see more rivalry in families where there are two or less years between siblings. When the siblings are the same sex, that increases the odds of jealous feelings. Dr. Emily Visher says that in those situations, parents tend to lump you into one. You're continually compared. In stepfamilies where there are two families joined together, it's even more difficult.

Measuring Love

When you try to measure love, you're almost always disappointed. What you have to understand, though, is that it's impossible for parents to treat their kids exactly the same. Love and attention don't get doled out in equal portions. The most you may be able to hope for is that they balance out over time. Your parents probably do love you. They just might not know how to show it.

Up Close

You should realize that you *are* experiencing a lot of change and pressure in your life. If you're feeling upset, you're normal. If you're taking out your emotions on a sister or brother, that's not so unusual, either. What you also have to remember is that everybody else in the family is going through lots of changes, too. And, as said previously, how each individual acts and feels bounces off the rest.

With that in mind, let's look at Kimberly and Essence again. What's going on with Kimberly? How is she feeling about moving back in with her mother, her mother's new relationship, and her own prospects for the future? How does her mother feel about loving a man who drinks and beats her? What is Kimberly's father experiencing as he adjusts to yet another domestic relationship? How is he handling his most recent job change?

Why does Essence feel angry and left out? Can she think of examples of favoritism shown to her sisters and brothers? Is she competing for the time her mother spends with all the other kids, or are there particular ones who make her feel the most jealous? Is her stepfather pulling away, thinking that Essence's feelings are not his problem?

Time Together

To face these kinds of questions about your own life, you might want to talk to your parent. This should be a scheduled conversation, not something you scream at each other during the height of rage and pain. At this prearranged time, let your parent(s) know that there's a problem. Then state what you think it is. Maybe they're playing favorites, and that makes you feel—fill in the blank—unappreciated, mad, upset, ignored, whatever. You feel they don't like you, that they like your brother or sister better. That makes you more furious.

If the problem is sibling rivalry, you might suggest that you and your parent spend fifteen minutes together in the evenings. Parents sometimes forget that even the most sophisticated teenagers still like and need attention. If you can't go to a parent, you might turn to another adult with whom you can talk. Or you might even try to find something likable about this new family member, try to think about your relationship from that perspective.

With stepsiblings, the other kids are probably feeling the same way you are. And their parent isn't feeling that hot about the situation, either. It's great if adults reach out to try to solve this problem, but you also can do the reaching.

Feelings Versus Actions

This is a crucial point: You have to separate your feelings from your actions. You can have lots of emotions, but your behavior needs to be controlled. In other words, you can *think* about pinching your baby brother. You can *think* about slugging your sister. *You just can't do it.*

> *Says Kimberly, "My sister and I took turns staying with my mom and my dad. They didn't realize it, but I looked at it as—hey, you baby-sit for three months and I'll baby-sit for five. I was with my mother first. She had a younger boyfriend, Johnny. He was an alcoholic. He took*

74

medication. When he didn't take it, he would hit her.

"One time he hit me, my father found out and they got in a big fight.

" 'Whoa! I want the kids,' my dad said. 'If you want to go off with your teeny-bopper boy-friend, go.'

"So the day before Mother's Day, my mom took off. After that, I saw her every other Sunday."

"Shallie and I lived in an apartment with my dad. At the time, he was seeing a lady named Grace. He came home one day from work and said, 'How would you feel if I moved in with Grace?'

"By that time, I was a little more mature. I looked at my dad and said, 'Whatever you want to do. If it makes you happy, then let's go.'

"We moved into this mansion that Grace owned. She had two kids. Renee, the girl, was one year older than I was. Damon, the boy, was one year younger than Shallie. We were very close in age, but they were snobby.

"Living with those other kids hurt my relationship with my sister, because she started seeing Damon. All of him, if you get my drift. My sister and Renee became best friends, and the thing with my sister and Damon heated up more. The only time me and Shallie ever talked was late at night and it was about my mom. The next day it was like it didn't really happen.

"Things went bad for me. Grace wanted to change me totally. In the past I talked just to my father, my mother, and sister. All of a sudden, Grace expected me to talk to everybody.

Whole conversations with everybody. I didn't care; I just talked to my father. Grace didn't like that. I was moved to another table to eat by myself.

"They didn't know that Damon and Shallie were all over each other upstairs in the bedroom. They just thought it was 'cute,' 'cause they were close.

"Renee and Damon and Shallie, none of them liked me. In a way, I can see why. I had a bad attitude on life then. I didn't get along with many kids or adults. I thought the adults were trying to be a substitute for my mom and my dad. But then again, my sister and those kids really didn't try to like me, either.

"Usually after school I'd go right to my room. Lie on my bed. Look at pictures of my mom. Listen to the radio, go down for dinner, and after dinner I'd go back to my room.

"One day I found this big, leather horsewhip. I showed it to my sister and she started playing with it. She was smacking the ground next to my feet. I said, 'Stop, stop!' She smacked my leg with it and it hurt! I hit her and Grace came in. She yelled at me, not my sister.

"My leg was bleeding. Shallie really whacked it, even though she didn't mean to. If any kind of pain hit me, I turned it to anger and I took it out on people.

"Grace hit me and threw me on my bed. I snapped back. I hit her several times and pushed her head into a doorknob. We had to take her to the hospital.

"She told my father that I bit her and caused a blood clot. Well, I did not bite her. Right in

front of her, I said, 'Dad, why would I punch her and nail her head to a doorknob and bite her?' He couldn't answer that. Neither could Grace. Grace is now in a mental institution."

10

INTIMATE ENEMIES

Arguing and fighting among brothers and sisters could be called the all-American pastime. Except it's no fun. All the teenagers interviewed offered battle descriptions. You fight about the bathroom, the dishes, the phone, the television, and money. You fight about having to watch your little sister and about being watched by your older brother. You fight over clothes and how each other looks.

Here's the difference, however. Some of you have moved beyond the bickering stage. You're no longer roughhousing. Instead, you fight so much and so often that you don't remember exactly what you're fighting about, and it's escalated into violence.

When there is actual hurting going on, when people are injured, something is seriously wrong. Professor Kahn writes in his book, *The Sibling Bond,* that a high level of violence can often mean that you are hungry for love, affection, and attention. You pound on a sibling to feel better temporarily. "Fighting, punching, even drawing blood can help emotionally starved children and adolescents to know that they are alive, by drawing a reaction from a familiar and intimate enemy. Through pain, the child obtains a rudimentary statement from others: you are alive, you are real, you are being noticed."[1]

But this isn't the way it's supposed to be, say the experts. There shouldn't be that kind of fighting between you and a sibling. Most of you are frightened by your violence. You find it scary and overwhelming. You have the impulse to do it—we all do. We all want to slug someone at some point. But in your heart, you wish you could stop.

Violent Feelings

In some families, you're taught by your parents that you can have violent feelings, but you can't act on them. If you are acting on them, those parents are letting things go too far. When they don't intervene and stop the violence, you feel guilty and bad about hurting your siblings. Then you get mad at yourself for feeling bad, and in anger you become even more violent.

Acting violent makes you afraid of your own anger. You end up feeling that you're dangerous. You're starting life feeling out of control. As a result, as you grow older and perhaps marry, you may brutalize your spouse and children. The bullies and the batterers by age fourteen often remain the bullies and batterers in later life.

It doesn't have to be this way. In your heart, you really know that it is *not* okay to hurt your siblings. Even though a parent may permit it or ignore it, beating up a

79

brother or sister is still not okay. Sometimes you have to take the side of your conscience. You have to join up with the one who says, *"Don't do this."* Although it might feel good to do it, although you might be furious and want to do it, *don't*.

If you're on the receiving end of physical violence, make it clear to a parent what is going on and that you want help in calling it off. Yes, a parent should know what's happening. A parent should have stopped it long ago. Still, a parent is the first person to talk to.

If your mother, father, or guardian is unable or unwilling to help you end the sibling war, talk to an adult whom you like and trust. Explain your family situation. Ask that person to help you evaluate the seriousness of what's occurring and to look for steps that might be taken to change it.

It *is* very hard to break patterns and create a new family script. Families seem to prefer the familiar. If you try to alter what exists, the whole family might become very unhappy with you. That's why so many of you react by saying, *"I just want to get out of the house."* It's not so much that you want out of the house, it's that you want out of the current family script. You don't want to have to stay in the role you've had, a role where you really can't be anything different from what the family has always expected of you.

Find out what support services your school has and try one. There could be peer counselors who will listen to you and help you come up with possible solutions; peer mediators to help you resolve your conflicts before they turn violent; or special classes for students with problems. What you should know and remember is that you don't have to feel as if you are drowning in this dilemma. It's important to connect with people and deal with what's happening instead of running away or escaping through drugs or alcohol.

Jocelyn, the full-time baby-sitter for her brother, Jason, says, "My patience with my brother has never been very good. He brings out my temper. One time I had a bunch of friends over to keep me company while I baby-sat. By then, about tenth grade, when my mother'd go out and there were six guys sitting with me in the den, she'd just say, 'As long as the house is immaculate when I walk in the door, I don't care if you have a party or not.'

"That was our deal. I'm good at cleaning up, because I always had to clean up after Jason. Anyway, that night I'd finally forced him to bed and he was still crying and crying. His crying is the most annoying thing. So when I couldn't stand it any longer, I went charging up the stairs and flung his door open so hard the handle got stuck in the wall.

"I ran to his bed and I grabbed him. I grabbed his shoulders and started screaming, 'Stop crying before I kill you!' He looked like a giant rag doll.

"One of the guys came running into the room and said, 'Jocelyn, Jocelyn, what are you doing? Stop shaking him!'

"It was like one of those really bad days."

The Case of the Stolen Earrings

After Anne-Marie's mother kicked the teenager's brother out of the house, Anne-Marie thought her problems were over. But she was wrong. Anne-Marie realized that stuff began to disappear from the room she shared with her fourteen-year-old sister, Pamela. One day her favorite gold hoop earrings were missing. Next she couldn't find her headset anywhere. Since she was almost positive Pamela had taken them, her first impulse was to scream at her sister or beat her up to make her confess.

Anne-Marie didn't want to go to her mother with this problem, because she felt her mother rarely listened. And even when she did listen, she was never much help. What Anne-Marie—or you—could try in a situation like this is a sibling variation of what's known as conflict or dispute resolution.

What might seem like a dumb approach to a fight is really a technique for channeling emotions, lowering pressure, and seeing problems more clearly. According to mediation experts Melissa Broderick and Michael Lewis, dispute resolution is often used by social service agencies, businesses, government, and schools as a way to end arguments before they lead to lawsuits, jail, conflict, or pain.

There are different ways to start. Read the following suggestions on various techniques to use to resolve conflicts more peacefully. If they seem like something that could work for you, check your library for books on this topic. There you'll find more detailed explanations.

To begin with, if you feel you're going to blow up, stop, take a deep breath, and count to ten. Then do that again. While this might seem silly and insignificant, it has two critical effects. Psychologically, it calms you down and helps you think more clearly. Physically, it slows your heartbeat and reduces the adrenaline racing through your system. The next steps take more time and can be done in any order.

I Wish You Were Dead

One technique has to do with practicing listening skills. Make up your mind that you're willing to listen to what your sister or brother has to say. Then give the person the space to explain his or her point of view. When people don't listen to you, you feel lousy, shut off, and not very important. Your sibling could be feeling that way, too.

Let's say you've told yourself you *will* listen to that sibling, only to hear a stream of abuse. You're supposed to stand around and do nothing while being put down and told off? Maybe your reaction is to retaliate with verbal attacks of your own. In Anne-Marie's case, she says she began shrieking at her sister, *"I can't believe you stole my earrings, you scum bag!!!! You're such a $@&* sister, I wish you were dead!"*

To which Pamela replied, *"Oh, yeah?! Well, get out of my face, you @#$&*+>!!!!! You're out,"* and then she shoved Anne-Marie.

By switching to neutral language and sentences that aren't filled with angry names, you avoid that instant hostility. Do this by turning your thoughts into "I statements." Begin with the words, "I'm feeling . . ." and then fill in the blank with whatever emotion you're experiencing at the moment.

I'm Feeling Really Upset

Anne-Marie might say, "I'm feeling really upset right now because I can't find my earrings and I think you might have them." Voicing concerns this way has a whole different tone. You're taking responsibility for your own feelings, rather than accusing the person who's made you angry.

What you also can do is write down what you'd say to a person you thought had hurt you in some way. These should be your exact complaints. Anne-Marie could write that she was angry at her sister because the missing earrings were her favorite. She worked as a checker at the grocery store, a job she didn't like, in order to earn money for her clothes and jewelry. She'd only had the earrings for a month. Everyone had told her how great they looked on her. Where did Pamela get off taking something that wasn't hers, especially something that meant so much to her? Was she going to have to hide stuff from her sister?

She wondered, too, if Pamela had taken them to trade for drugs. Or had she taken them because she was angry at Anne-Marie or their mother or life in general? Even if she was messed up, she had no right to steal from her very own sister.

Good Guy, Bad Guy

After writing down your complaints, read them over and ask yourself, what is the *real* issue behind all those words? What's beneath the surface of the fight? With Anne-Marie and Pamela, it might be about trust. They are sisters, and Anne-Marie might like to think that she can trust her sibling to ask before she takes something that doesn't belong to her. It could have to do with respect. Siblings should respect each other and each other's belongings. Or it might have to do with status. The gold hoop earrings made Anne-Marie feel good and important and sexy.

Once you've identified what the real issue is you have to say it in a sentence to the person with whom you're in conflict. Again use an "I statement." Anne-Marie could say something like this to her sister: "I'm feeling upset because I thought we had an understanding to ask first if we borrowed something from the other."

Truce

When tempers are cooler, you and a sibling might negotiate a truce to your war and make another list of all the horrible things you've called each other. Then compare your lists and talk about how you feel when someone says those things about you. You might discover that sometimes you can use the same language with each other in a joking way and it's okay. At other times, it really hurts, because it's meant to be mean and cause pain.

You could talk about how you'd like to be treated and what you like to be called. What are the positive things you like to hear about yourself? And what, if anything, have you been known to say about your sibling in a positive way? What makes that person a good sibling, in your opinion?

You could also set up guidelines for fighting. You know you can't manage to stop arguing entirely, but you can agree to rules. Only one person talks at a time—and with no interrupting. The person who's talking says what he or she thinks went on. Then the other person tells his or her story.

Next you both try to decide what's really going on. By using "I statements" and summarizing and rephrasing each other's point of view, you begin to identify the underlying issues. You talk through what's gone on, why it's gone on, and what you want to do to change things. Finally, you figure out where you want to go from here. What do you want to do about this problem? Can you come to an understanding?

Peace Treaty

In some cases, you might want to record this understanding by writing an agreement. Then and there come up with a statement that you both feel you can live with. Agree to stick to it. This type of conflict resolution is often easier to do if you have a third or fourth person involved. For example, you could ask another sibling or a friend to help you solve a particular problem.

That person or persons would act as mediator. They would remind you of the rules—no interrupting, one turn at a time, tell your story. They would also help clarify what's being said. They might say to Anne-Marie: You're saying that your sister stole your earrings, and she's saying she didn't. She just borrowed them without asking because she knew you'd say no if she asked. And then she lost them. That's not the same as stealing.

The two sisters would then either on their own or with the help of the mediator decide what to do. Pamela feels bad because she lost the earrings, but she can't replace them since she has no job and no money. She was afraid to admit what happened since she knows Anne-Marie has a temper. But she didn't have anything to do with the missing headset and was hurt that Anne-Marie immediately decided she had traded it for drugs.

What's happening here is that the two sisters are *talking*. That might not seem important unless you realize that you can't solve a problem without communication and a willingness to try to come to an agreement. The exact wording doesn't matter, but the spirit of what they write down is that neither will borrow any property from the other without first asking permission, and then it must be returned the same day and in the same condition. In addition, Pamela has to make Anne-Marie's bed and clean up the entire room instead of just her own part for the next month to repay Anne-Marie for the lost earrings. Case closed. (The missing headset was later found wedged between the wall and Anne-Marie's bed, hidden by a pile of clothes.)

11

PROBLEM SOLVING

Although Armando now lives in a house full of brothers, until he was ten, he was an only child.

"Before my mother remarried, she had to work because my father disappeared and didn't pay support. I was dependent on her, but what with her working day and night, she wasn't really there. Where we lived once, it didn't have any heat. It was a cold-water flat.

"The only luxuries we had would be to have dessert before dinner. Or my mother would throw all the lawn chairs in the back of the car and take me and my friends to the drive-in movie. Whenever my mother could, she would spend time with me. She gave up her whole youth for me. Back then I wanted a brother or sister, someone to play with, even someone to fight with.

"When she married Tony, he got custody of Xavier and Desmond, his two kids from another marriage; they all moved in with us, too. But I didn't know how to share. And 'Xavier, the oldest, liked my clothes and games better than his own. Desmond, he was younger, but he was bigger than me. He called me names.

"He'd say, 'You're such an idiot. How'd you get so stupid?' He'd call me 'imbecile' and 'dog-breath' and words you wouldn't put in a book. He'd say the most I'd ever be was a bag person, then he'd say, 'can picker, can picker' at me when I was taking down the garbage.

"He picked on me and then he used the excuse, 'Xavier picks on me.' I tried to ignore him, but he just kept going. Then I tried to yell at him and that just got me more upset. I didn't understand why he did it. Didn't he know it hurt?"

Backward Behavior

Some experts say that when it comes to people learning how to act toward each other, it's often done backward. Instead of being aware of good behavior, bad behavior is what gets all the attention. For example, whenever Jocelyn takes her brother, Jason, to the corner store, once inside he starts carrying on, demanding ice cream. When she doesn't buy him any, he lies on the floor, kicks his feet, and screams. To keep him quiet, Jocelyn gives in and buys him a treat. What she's doing is letting him know that if he misbehaves, he'll be rewarded.

Praise is a more effective way of modifying behavior.

What you really want to do is to catch people doing something positive and then compliment them. Maybe you think that one of your siblings is your parent's favorite. First, ask yourself why you think that's true. What exactly is that person doing that leads you to believe there is favoritism? Can you find examples of your parent's favoritism to show how truthful your feelings are?

Changing Behavior

Let's look at a situation where your parents yell at you and not at your brother or sister. Now how could you modify that behavior? From your own experiences, think of something that would encourage your mother or father to say something nice to you. In order to change their behavior, you are getting them to do something that makes you feel good and then complimenting them. You might be pleasantly surprised at the reaction.

When Armando is tormented by his brother, Desmond, he feels the words rain down on him like fists. What can he do to stop this verbal violence? The experts suggest that first Armando should analyze the circumstances. When does the teasing occur? Where does it occur? What starts it? What happens when the teasing becomes painful? What does Armando do first? Second? How can he change his behavior in order to change his sibling's behavior? What kinds of actions would you suggest?

Hard as it might be, try doing something nice for whomever is the source of the problem. Begin working for change simply by saying something kind, thanking the sibling for something he or she did, or paying a compliment. In Armando's case, one day he noticed Desmond was shooting hoops. After watching a while, he casually said, "You have one fine hook shot, Desmond. I really wish I could do that, too." Desmond offered to show him how, and then for three days, he didn't verbally attack Armando.

If that technique doesn't work, you may have to look for ways to avoid the problem. Once Armando kept his cool by removing himself from the skirmish. He stopped participating. He went into the bathroom, locked the door, and didn't come out until Desmond had left. Look at your own behavior. Are you doing something that brings out the worst in your sibling? Can you stop or change that behavior, taking away any excuse for your sibling's attack? It's not fair to put the burden on you, but it may bring about the end of the war.

Sexual Curiosity

You can't change your family all by yourself. You need help. Help can come from the other members of your family or it can come from outside. As you read in Chapter 8, it's vital to find an understanding, sympathetic adult and tell that person you need help. Especially if there is sexual or physical abuse in your home, find an adult you trust and let that person know what is happening.

There is a line between sexual curiosity and sexual contact that siblings should not cross. Dealing with this boundary between stepbrothers and stepsisters is tricky. You may not be related by blood, but you are related by your parent's marriage. You *are* a family unit. Lines should be drawn by your parents, because if they aren't, you may start feeling increasingly anxious. Dr. Emily Visher says that this is another situation where feelings of sexual curiosity and attraction are normal and okay, but you just can't act on them. It's too complicated.

If you're confronted by a new stepsibling who's about

your age and who shares your interests, why shouldn't there be an attraction? But when you're living in the same home, a romantic relationship must be off limits. Sexual interest often takes the form of teasing or anger. In a way, it's safer to argue than to face the fact that you have these warm feelings. So you control your affection by fighting.

If the situation makes you uncomfortable, talk to your parent. Maybe you could phrase it in terms of wanting more privacy. See if you can change your bedroom so there's more distance between the two of you. See if there's any way you don't have to share a bathroom. You want to take the focus off the sexual part.

Sexual Violence

It's estimated that one of every five females has been or will be sexually abused as a child by a family member.[1] Experts also believe that sibling incest—sex between biological siblings—may be the most common and underreported form of incest there is. Some estimate that sibling incest occurs five times as often as the more frequently discussed father-daughter incest.[2] A male member of the family can also be sexually abused.

Sexual curiosity about a brother or sister is not unusual. It's not even that unusual for there to be physical contact. But when you're not very close in age—more than three or four years between you—and you go beyond normal exploration, for example, there is oral-genital contact or intercourse, that is sexual violence. And just as with the batterer, the brother who is sexually abusing his sister when they're both kids could easily become the adult sex offender.

The experts sometimes divide sibling incest into two types: power-oriented and nurture-oriented. Power-oriented usually means an older sibling is forcing a younger one to have sex. With nurture-oriented incest, it's mutual, the two hold on to each other as a defense against a stormy home life.

Either kind of incest happens more often in families where parents aren't paying much attention to you. In a sense, they've abandoned you, at least emotionally, and possibly in reality, too. You feel that they aren't there for you when you need them. These parents are distant, inaccessible. There may be family secrets—of alcoholism, drug abuse, parent-child incest. In some situations, where you wish for a loving parent, some of you may settle for a loving sister or brother. You offer each other comfort and a way to express bitter feelings and even fury.

Sibling incest is a grave problem. There are books on this issue. If you want more information before seeking help, take one out from your library. Victim/survivors of incest feel numb, betrayed, angry, and guilty. The perpetrators—the ones who commit the crime—must accept responsibility for what's happening and apologize. They have to learn how to control their behavior and develop a sense of self without using force. Both the survivors and the perpetrators must learn how to value themselves. These are hard lessons to come by without a trained professional showing the way.

12

BACK TO THE FUTURE

As you read this book, you met some of the teenagers interviewed while exploring the issue of sibling relationships. I would have liked to have gone back to them after I questioned the experts. I'd say, here are the experts' suggestions. Would you try these ideas for six months and let me know if you're getting along any better with your sister or brother?

But that wasn't possible. What I did do, though, was to track down the main kids you heard from on these pages. We talked by phone and discussed what changes, if any, there had been in this area of their life since our earlier conversations. Here's what I found.

Darnell and Cherisse

I couldn't locate Darnell and his sister Cherisse. During the last two years, they'd lived with an aunt and her family, their mother in a shelter, another aunt, and then their grandmother. It was her phone number I had for them, and it was disconnected. The intermediate school they attended said that Darnell was no longer enrolled and Cherisse had graduated.

Bonnie

Bonnie, the girl whose three older sisters had hit her and stolen from her, says nothing has changed. She doesn't expect it to. Her only hope, she feels, lies in focusing on the distant future.

> *Sometimes when it gets too much for me, I call my best friend and yell at her. She doesn't like my sisters either, so she understands. If I were my parents, I don't know what I'd do to make things better. I don't try to analyze it. I really don't know if anything can be done. We just don't like each other. My mom knows how I feel; and I think it's pretty clear that I'll feel the same when we're older. Ten years from now, I want to have moved far, far away from them. Wherever they are, I don't want to be.*

Jocelyn

Jocelyn is much more optimistic. She still believes that the fabric of her family was ripped apart when her father left. Now that she's older and wiser and getting ready for college, she understands that her parents didn't divorce to torment her. And they tried hard to make the best of their new situation. There simply

95

wasn't the money available to pay for day-care for her baby brother. What Jocelyn did on her own was gather her friends around her for support in weathering these emotional storms.

My friends say I used to be a very insecure person. I always needed someone to be there. Lately, I figured out that overnight I went from being that insecure kid to being my little brother's mother and father, and being my mother's mother and her sister, too. My friends and my boyfriend helped me a lot. Now I have more freedom. I have my own car. I have my own phone and my own answering machine. I'm looking forward to college where I want to study retail business management. I want to be somebody big at a department store like Macy's.

Armando

Armando's story also comes with a happier ending. In this case, his mother and stepfather halted the warfare. They finally saw what damage the fighting was creating. When Armando nearly smothered his baby brother, they called a family meeting. Armando explains:

They said that starting right then, every weekend night unless we're having baseball practice we would eat dinner together. No excuses. After the meal, we can all say what we want. Everybody can just jump in and start talking about whatever. Everybody has to listen to what everybody has to say.

My mom and my 'dad-now' say that commu-

96

nication is the most important thing. We have to tell each other how we really feel, even with them. Like if they're yelling at us, we can tell them how we feel about them yelling at us. We don't yell back at them, we just tell them. "Mom, I didn't like it—it hurt my feelings— when you did such and such to me." They taught us how to say things like that. Or if two of us are really going at each other, they might talk to us together later. They ask us if we could be a little kinder and not so mean to each other. We're learning to solve our problems.

I'm not saying everything is perfect. It isn't. But things have calmed down. A couple months ago, my parents got a separate telephone line for us kids. Now sometimes my mother calls me from her number at eleven at night and we talk for an hour. It's easier to talk to her on the phone. We can't always talk face to face because we get on each other's nerves. But on the phone, we have our good times. Just me and her. Then before she hangs up, she says, "Armando, don't ever forget that you'll always be my first."

Kimberly

Kimberly is as talkative as she'd been before. She sent her sister a letter, she tells me.

I wrote, "We've had our ins and outs, but I remember the times when we would lie in bed and you'd listen to the little jokes I told and laugh even when they weren't funny. That's being a real sister."

When I was younger, Shallie was a real sis-
ter. But during the time we were both maturing,
she wasn't a sister anymore. She was just like a
person I was acquainted with. That hurt. When
she read what I wrote her, she called. I said,
"Why don't you write me back?"

She said, "You wrote me a six-page letter!"

I thought, wow! Here I'd taken all that time
to write her and what does she do but complain
about the length. When you have a sister like
mine, you really don't want to be like her. She's
great, and I love her to death, but we still fight.
We still don't get along. The words "I love you"
come out seldom.

I look at my sister's life: she's twenty years
old. She doesn't have her license. She doesn't
have a car. She doesn't even have a job. What is
she going to do in a couple years? Is her whole
life about looking for the next boyfriend?

I have my license. I'm getting a car. And I'm
only seventeen. I guarantee you, I know where
I'm going. When I finish high school, I'm going
back to Wisconsin, hang out there for the sum-
mer. I want to see what's going on with the boy-
friend I left behind. But I know that nothing
lasts forever.

I want to go to college and then I want to
become a flight engineer in the navy. By the
time I'm thirty-two, I'll have everything I've
ever wanted. I know that no matter how bad
things get, or how bad I'm in a hole, up top
there's something great waiting for me.

Throughout my growing-up years, I always
thought my dad and my mom and my sister
were first on my list. I did everything I could to
please them. No matter what I did, I got hurt.

Now I've learned that I've got to put myself first. I'm a very determined person. I'm not going to go without ever again.

Just as Kimberly and I are getting ready to end our phone call, I can hear an argument in the background. Her father and his woman-friend are fighting. She's telling him he's out the door and he had better take his daughter with him. Kimberly says she has to hang up and the phone goes dead.

Essence

My final conversation with Essence is brief. One foster brother, the oldest, is leaving, but some Japanese exchange students are due the next day to stay for three weeks. "My stepfather thinks we ought to put in a revolving door," she says, before adding that nothing much has changed since we last talked. Sometimes she writes poetry to work out her feelings on some of the issues. She promises to send me copies of her favorites.

Anne-Marie

The changes that have taken place in Anne-Marie's life are the biggest surprise. She is married, has a baby, and is trying to continue in school. "The future is where I'm looking, not the past," she says.

I never want to see my brother again. My husband doesn't understand, but he doesn't know I was raped by my brother. I don't think he could accept that fact. It has to be my secret. My sis-

ter? Because I'm out of the house, she's not a problem anymore.

Your Connection

Your connection with your sisters and brothers is often life's longest lasting relationship. You may go separate ways, live in different cities, pick different careers. This relationship, though, is one to which most people return.

When experts surveyed adults over sixty-five, they discovered that about half of them saw at least one sibling each week. And almost all of them valued the connection enough to continue the relationship by phone, mail, or personal contact—even if they didn't see each other that often.[1]

Your siblings are the people who really know you. You share a collective history that you don't have with other people. Suddenly, you will be reminded of a day years ago when you were both kids. You smile. With time and distance, the intensity of your emotions has cooled.

With siblings, you can always touch base and feel the reassurance that comes from someone who's been there forever. For better or worse, you all know the family secrets. Right now you cannot imagine wanting to see a sibling again. But in later years, you might be surprised. Think about it. That brother or sister you're fighting with, have no time for, and can't stand may turn out to be a very good friend.

NOTE: I'd like to hear from you about your sibling problems. If you try any of the solutions, please let me know about that, too. Write me at this address:

Janet Bode
c/o FRANKLIN WATTS
387 Park Avenue South
New York, New York 10016

PANEL OF EXPERTS

Joanne Althoff, M.S.W., a clinical social worker with a private practice in Baltimore, Maryland, spends much of her time counseling couples and families going through divorce. Prior to that, she served as director of the Sexual Assault Program at Baltimore City Hospital. She was especially helpful in the parts of this book dealing with sexuality among siblings and the effects of divorce on children. Althoff is the oldest of two sisters and says that they didn't really know each other when they were growing up. "We liked each other, but we didn't confide —even though we're just two years apart. Now, though, I talk to my sister long distance at least every other week."

Neil Bernstein, Ph.D., an only child, says that he can remember always wishing he had an older sibling to guide him. Today he's doing the guiding. He's a clinical psychologist specializing in adolescents and families, with offices in Washington, D.C., and Alexandria, Virginia. He often appears as a panelist on TV talk shows, and writes for professional journals, including the article, "How Parents Can Deal with Sibling Rivalry." His thoughts are reflected in the sections that discuss the relation between siblings at war and parents who fuel it. Because he also believes that teenagers can't handle serious family problems single-handedly, he offers advice on how to proceed.

Carol Bloom, C.S.W., a New York City therapist, is a cofounder of the Women's Therapy Centre Institute, which specializes in women's psychology and eating problems. Her approach to food and eating can be found in Chapter 8. She's a middle child with a sister who's four and a half years older and a brother who's fifteen months younger. "When we were kids," says Bloom, "I was closer to my brother and looked up to my sister. She was Miss Everything. Now I talk to both of them once if not twice a week."

Melissa Broderick, M.Ed., is the program director of the Children's Hearings Project of Cambridge Family and Children's Service, Cambridge, Massachusetts. The staff of this organization began the first parent-child mediation program in the country. Today they also run training programs nationwide to teach students how to mediate disputes between one another and settle conflicts before they turn violent. Some of the techniques they use are described in Chapter 10. When her own siblings are mentioned, Broderick laughs. She's the youngest of five, with three older sisters and one older brother. "I began to study mediation at the dinner table," she says. "Now we're more able to hash things out than when we were children."

Because Paul Coiteux's (Ph.D.) one sister is nine years older, she wasn't around much when he was growing up. In many ways, he felt as if they were two only children. Now, he says, they're very close and see each other a couple of times a month. This school psychologist for Wappingers Central School District, New York, keeps a shrunken head in his office. When students come in to see the "shrink," Dr. Coiteux is ready to listen and offer advice. He works with them to come up with ways to change their own behavior and that of those around them, following the methods in Chapter 11. Outside of school, Dr. Coiteux sees clients in his private practice and lectures at a state university, S.U.N.Y.–New Paltz, New York.

Ed Farrar, M.A., divides his time among three positions. He's a licensed marriage, family, and child counselor with a private practice; the clinical supervisor at the Family Service Association of Santa Cruz, California; and a consulting therapist for a group home. He encourages teens to see that sibling problems are part of a total picture: the father yells at the older son who punches the younger son who kicks the dog who bites the mailman. When asked about siblings, Farrar says, "I was lucky. I didn't have any, but I lived next door to my best friend, who was in a family of five. I got to go on vacations with them, but at Christmas, I got all the presents."

Dan Gottfried, M.S.W., is an only male, the second-born, with four sisters. When he was in his late teens, he acquired two more sisters, stepsisters this time. "I always wanted a B-O-Y, a brother," he says. Today he has two jobs. During the school year, he's a psychological counselor at Putnam-Northern Westchester B.O.C.E.S. in New York. In the summer he directs a Unitarian-Universalist camp, Unirondack. His approach to teenagers is to be absolutely up front with them. His request for this book: Please help kids find ways to cope with life in *real* families, not in some ideal family that's nothing like where they're living. He was particularly good at explaining family scripts and how to deal with sibling violence.

Margaret Hayner, C.S.W., is a family therapist in private practice on Long Island, New York, and is affiliated with the Malvern Center for Family Therapy. You can see her thoughts expressed especially in the sections that cover family scripts and families that are out of control. She is convinced that people can change and respond more positively to each other. Professionally and personally, she has spent a lot of time dealing with sibling issues. She has three older sisters and one younger brother. Hayner says, "Even though I come from a big family, I found plenty of ways of making myself heard."

Michael Jacobson, Ph.D., is the founder and executive director of the consumer advocacy organization, Center for Science in the Public Interest (CSPI). Not only has he been a leader in the fast-food reform movement, he has also worked for healthier food preparation and ingredient labeling so people know what they're eating. When he was a kid he "got along swimmingly" with his sister, who is two years older. At the age of ten, though, his family changed to include two stepsisters and a stepbrother. "We survived our sibling rivalry, and now that we're adults, our relationships are fine," says Dr. Jacobson.

Michael D. Kahn, Ph.D., is the only child of two only children and he married an only child. That's why, he says, he became interested in the topic of brothers and sisters and has devoted much of his career to researching their relationships. In fact, he is now one of the nation's authorities on sibling relationships. He's the coauthor/editor of two books on siblings, *The Sibling Bond* written with Stephen P. Bank, Ph.D., and *Siblings in Therapy* written with Karen Gail Lewis, Ed.D., as well as a psychology professor at the University of Hartford, Connecticut. Dr. Kahn believes that rivalry is not necessarily the norm. The focus on it, in his opinion, is because Sigmund Freud was an oldest child who couldn't stand his younger siblings.

Michael Lewis, J.D., a lawyer and mediator, is a senior adviser to the National Institute on Dispute Resolution in Washington, D.C. The purpose of this organization is to help people better understand how to solve problems. It also provides funds to others to teach these dispute-resolution methods. Some of the approaches can be found in Chapter 10. Lewis has a sister who is three years younger. "She was pretty much a nonperson in my life when we were kids. We didn't have a relationship. However, we now both live in Washington and talk once a week."

Peter Thomashow, M.D., is a New York City psychiatrist who specializes in biofeedback and behavioral medicine. Many of his patients come to see him about long-term problems such as chronic headaches, pain disorders, insomnia—ailments where the body has been adversely affected by stress. He then teaches them biofeedback and meditation techniques. For this book, he provided valuable assistance on the chapters that cover stress and pressure, and how to reduce their impact on your body and emotions. Dr. Thomashow has one brother, three years older, who "was and still is my best friend."

Emily B. Visher, Ph.D., a psychologist, and John S. Visher, M.D., a psychiatrist, are the founders of the Stepfamily Association of America and the authors of three books on stepfamilies, including *How to Win as a Stepfamily*. This Los Altos Hills, California, husband-and-wife team gained hands-on experience with siblings and stepsiblings when they married. Each came with four children. They offer unique insight into sibling problems when there has been a divorce and remarriage. Dr. Emily Visher is an oldest child with two younger brothers, one of whom is deceased. Dr. John Visher is also an oldest of four boys and ". . . proud of them all," he says, before admitting that they have a better relationship today than they did when they were kids.

SOURCE NOTES

Chapter 2
1. Judy Dunn, *Sisters and Brothers* (Cambridge, MA: Harvard University Press, 1985) p. 4.

Chapter 3
1. Stephen P. Bank and Michael D. Kahn, *The Sibling Bond* (New York: Basic Books, 1982), p. 63.
2. Ibid., p. 69.

Chapter 5
1. Population Reference Bureau, personal conversation, 9 January 1990.
2. AP wire service, "Hungry Children Increase in Survey," *New York Times,* 21 December 1989. National Section.
3. Ibid.
4. Mary Cronin, Melissa Ludtke and Sylvester Monroe, "Our Violent Kids," *Time,* 12 June 1989, p. 54. (According to 1987 statistics, poverty in America was de-

fined as household income below $11,611 for a family of four.)

5. Bill McAllistor, "The Menaced Lives of Black Men," *Newsday,* 3 January 1990, National Section. (According to Center on Budget and Policy Priorities, in 1987 the number of African-American children under eighteen living in poverty was 45.6 percent.)

6. Julie Johnson, "Mental Disorders Measured in Young," *New York Times,* 8 June 1989. News Section. (According to a study by the Institute of Medicine, 12 percent of the nation's population under eighteen suffer from a mental disorder or emotional disturbance. Among the poor, the problem is worse—20 percent. Poverty, homelessness, and growing up in crowded, inner-city neighborhoods are cited as causes.)

7. Lawrence Kutner, "In Blended Families, Rivalry Intensifies," *New York Times,* 5 January 1989, Parent and Child Section.

8. Ibid.

Chapter 6

1. In addition to some of the experts personally interviewed, these author/experts held this opinion: Margaret H. Hoopes and James Harper, *Birth Order Roles and Sibling Patterns in Individual and Family Therapy* (Rockville, MD: Aspen Publishers, 1987); Clifford E. Isaacson, *Understanding Yourself Through Birth Order* (Algona, Iowa: Upper Des Moines Counseling Service, 1988); Kevan Leman, *The Birth Order Book: Why You Are the Way You Are* (Old Tappan, N.J.: F.H. Revell, 1985); Bradford Wilson and George Edington, *First Child, Second Child . . . Your Birth Order Profile* (New York: McGraw-Hill, 1981).

2. Michael D. Kahn and Karen Gail Lewis, editors, *Siblings in Therapy: Life Span and Clinical Issues* (New York: Norton, 1988), p. xviii. ("While we deplore the

110

books which fuel popular myths with unsubstantiated [and linear] speculations about [. . . birth order], they seem to linger in the public mind.")

Chapter 7
1. "Life Change Index Scale" developed by Drs. Thomas Holmes and Richard Rahe.

Chapter 8
1. Michael F. Jacobson and Sarah Fritschner, *The Fastfood Guide: What's Good, What's Bad and How to Tell the Difference* (New York: Workman Publishing, 1986), p. 79.

Chapter 10
1. Stephen P. Bond and Michael D. Kahn, *The Sibling Bond* (New York: Basic Books), p. 198–9.

Chapter 11
1. Carol Poston and Karen Lison, *Reclaiming Our Lives: Hope for Adult Survivors of Incest* (Boston: Little, Brown & Co., 1989), jacket.
2. Michael D. Kahn and Karen Gail Lewis, editors, *Siblings in Therapy: Life Span and Clinical Issues* (New York: Norton, 1988), p. 11.

Chapter 12
1. Ibid, p. 415.

BIBLIOGRAPHY

Sibling and related issues

(All Young Adult [YA] titles are marked.)

Ames, Louise Bates. *He Hit Me First*. New York: W.W. Norton, 1982. (YA)

Arnold, Joan Hagan. *A Child Dies: A Portrait of Family Grief*. Rockville, MD.: Aspen Systems Corp., 1983.

Bank, Stephen P. and Michael D. Kahn. *The Sibling Bond*. New York: Basic Books, 1982.

Barbeau, Clayton. *How to Raise Parents: Questions and Answers for Teens and Parents*. San Francisco: Harper & Row, 1987. (YA)

Beer, William R., editor. *Relative Strangers: Studies of Stepfamily Process*. Totowa, N.J.: Rowman & Littlefield, 1988.

Beer, William R. *Strangers in the House: The World of Stepsiblings and Half-Siblings*. New Brunswick, N.J.: Transaction Publishers, 1989.

Blake, Judith. *Family Size and Achievement.* Berkeley: University of California Press, 1989.

Blume, Judy. *Superfudge.* New York: E.P. Dutton, 1980. (YA)

Coyne, John. *Brothers and Sisters.* New York: E.P. Dutton, 1985.

Craven, Linda. *Stepfamilies: New Patterns of Harmony.* New York: Julian Messner, 1982. (YA)

Dunn, Judy. *Sisters and Brothers.* Cambridge, MA.: Harvard University Press, 1985.

Faber, Adele and Elaine Mazlish. *Siblings without Rivalry.* New York: W.W. Norton, 1987.

Festinger, Trudy Bradley. *No One Ever Asked Us: Postscript to Foster Care.* New York: Columbia University Press, 1983.

Garbarino, James and Cynthia J. Schellenback, Janet M. Sebes, et al. *Troubled Youth, Troubled Families: Understanding Families at Risk for Adolescent Maltreatment.* New York: Aldine Publishing Co., 1986.

Getzoff, Ann, and Carolyn McClenahan. *Stepkids: A Survival Guide for Teenagers in Stepfamilies.* New York: Walker and Co., 1984. (YA)

Gilbert, Sara. *Trouble at Home.* New York: Lothrop, Lee and Shephard Books, 1981. (YA)

Goode, Stephen. *Violence in America.* New York: Julian Messner, 1984. (YA)

Hellmuth, Jerome. *Coping with Parents.* New York: The Rosen Publishing Group, 1985. (YA)

Hoopes, Margaret H., and James Harper. *Birth Order Roles and Sibling Patterns in Individual and Family Therapy.* Rockville, MD.: Aspen Publishers, 1987.

Hyde, Margaret O. *Is This Kid "Crazy?": Understanding Unusual Behavior.* Philadelphia: The Westminster Press, 1983. (YA)

Isaacson, Clifford E. *Understanding Yourself through*

Birth Order. Algona, Iowa: Upper Des Moines Counseling Center, 1988.

Kahn, Michael D., and Karen Gail Lewis, editors. *Siblings in Therapy: Life Span and Clinical Issues.* New York: W.W. Norton, 1988.

Keshet, Jamie. *Love and Power in the Stepfamily: A Practical Guide.* New York: McGraw-Hill, 1987.

Kiell, Norman, editor. *Blood Brothers: Siblings as Writers.* New York: International Universities Press, 1983.

Kosoff, Anna. *Incest: Families in Crisis.* New York: Franklin Watts, 1985. (YA)

Lamb, Michael E., and Brian Sutton-Smith, editors. *Sibling Relationships: Their Nature and Significance across the Lifespan.* Hillsdale, N.J.: L. Erlbaum Associates, 1982.

Leman, Kevin. *The Birth Order Book: Why You Are the Way You Are.* Old Tappan, N.J.: F.H. Revell, 1985.

McConville, Brigid. *Sisters: Love and Conflict within the Lifelong Bond.* London: Pan Books, 1985.

McGoldrick, M., and J. Pearce, J. Giordano, editors. *Ethnicity and Family Therapy.* New York: Guildford, 1982.

Meltzer, Milton. *Poverty in America.* New York: William Morrow & Co., 1986. (YA)

Meyer, Donald J., and Patricia F. Vadasy, Rebecca R. Fewell. *Living with a Brother or Sister with Special Needs: A Book for Sibs.* Seattle: University of Washington Press, 1985.

Powell, Thomas H., and Peggy Ahrenhold Ogle. *Brothers and Sisters: A Special Part of Exceptional Families.* Baltimore: Brookes Publishing Co., 1985.

Richards, Arlene, and Irene Willis. *How to Get it Together When Your Parents Are Coming Apart.* New York: David McKay Company, 1976. (YA)

Rosen, Helen. *Unspoken Grief: Coping with Childhood Sibling Loss.* Lexington, MA.: Lexington Books, 1986.

Ryan, Elizabeth A. *Straight Talk about Parents.* New York: Facts on File, 1989. (YA)

Stark, Evan. *Everything You Need to Know about Family Violence.* New York: The Rosen Publishing Group, Inc. 1989. (YA)

Toman, Walter. *Family Constellation: Its Effects on Personality and Social Behavior.* New York: Springer Publishing Co., 1976.

Visher, Emily, and John Visher. *How to Win as a Stepfamily.* Chicago: Contemporary Books, 1982.

Wallerstein, Judith S., and Sandra Blakeslee. *Second Chances: Men, Women and Children a Decade After Divorce.* New York: Ticknor & Fields, 1989.

Wilson, Bradford, and George Edington. *First Child, Second Child . . . Your Birth Order Profile.* New York: McGraw-Hill, 1981.

Worth, Richard. *The American Family.* New York: Franklin Watts, 1984. (YA)

Zukow, Patricia Goldring, editor. *Sibling Interaction across Cultures: Theoretical and Methodological Issues.* New York: Springer-Verlag, 1989.

Mediation

Beer, Jennifer E. *Peacemaking in Your Neighborhood: Reflections on an Experiment in Community Mediation.* Philadelphia, PA.: New Society Publishers, 1986.

Fisher, Roger, and William Ury. *Getting to Yes: Negotiating Agreement without Giving In.* New York: Penguin Books, 1983.

Irving, Howard H., and Michael Benjamin. *Family Mediation: Theory and Practice of Dispute Resolution.* Toronto: Carswell, 1987.

Kreidler, William J. *Creative Conflict Resolution: More Than 200 Activities for Keeping Peace in the Classroom.* Glenview, IL.: Scott, Foresman, 1984.

Moore, Christopher W. *The Mediation Process: Practical Strategies for Resolving Conflict.* San Francisco: Jossey-Bass, 1986.

Wright, Martin, and Burt Galaway, editors. *Mediation and Criminal Justice: Victims, Offenders and Community.* London; Newbury Park, CA.: Sage Publications, 1988.

Meditation

Aitken, Robert. *Taking the Path of Zen.* San Francisco: North Point Press, 1982.

Bielefeldt, Carl. *Dogen's Manuals of Zen Meditation.* Berkeley: University of California Press, 1988.

Chogyam, Ngakga. *Journey into Vastness: A Handbook of Tibetan Meditation Techniques.* Shaftesbury, England: Element, 1988.

Da, Liu. *T'ai Chi Ch'uan and Meditation.* New York: Schocken Books, 1986.

Weiss, Anne E. *Biofeedback: Fact or Fad?* New York: Franklin Watts, 1984. (YA)

Nutrition and Body Image

Bowen-Woodward, Kathy. *Coping with a Negative Body Image.* New York: The Rosen Publishing Group, Inc., 1989. (YA)

Brody, Jane. *Jane Brody's Good Food Book.* New York: W.W. Norton, 1985.

Eagles, Douglas A. *Nutritional Diseases.* New York: Franklin Watts, 1987. (YA)

Jacobson, Michael F., and Sarah Fritschner. *The Fast-food Guide: What's Good, What's Bad, and How to Tell the Difference.* New York: Workman Publishing, 1986.

Jacobson, Michael F. *The Complete Eater's Digest and Nutrition Scoreboard.* Garden City, N.Y.: Anchor Press, 1985.

Liebman, Bonnie et al. *Salt: The Brand Name Guide to Sodium Content.* New York: Warner Books, 1983.

Orbach, Susie. *Fat Is a Feminist Issue: The Anti-diet Guide to Permanent Weight Loss.* New York: Paddington Press, 1978.

————. *Fat Is a Feminist Issue II: A Program to Conquer Compulsive Eating.* New York: Berkley Books, 1982.

Orlandi, Mario, and Donald Prue with Annette Spence. *Encyclopedia of Good Health: Nutrition.* New York: Facts on File, 1989. (YA)

Stress

American Health Magazine editors with Daniel Goleman, Tara Benett-Goleman and Judith Groch. *The Relaxed Body Book: A High-Energy Anti-tension Program.* Garden City, N.Y.: Doubleday, 1986.

Antonovsky, Aaron. *Unraveling the Mystery of Health: How People Manage Stress and Stay Well.* San Francisco: Jossey-Bass, 1987.

Damon, William, and Daniel Hart. *Self-understanding in Childhood and Adolescence.* New York: Cambridge University Press, 1988.

Elkind, David. *All Grown Up and No Place to Go: Teenagers in Crisis.* Reading, MA.: Addison-Wesley, 1984.

Humphrey, James H. *Children and Stress: Theoretical Perspectives and Recent Research.* New York: AMS Press, 1988.

————, editor. *Stress in Childhood.* New York: AMS Press, 1984.

Johnson, James H. *Life Events as Stressors in Childhood and Adolescence.* Newbury Park, CA.: Sage Publications, 1986.

McCubbin, Hamilton I. and A. Elizabeth Cauble, Joan M. Patterson, editors. *Family Stress, Coping, and Social Support.* Springfield, IL.: Thomas, 1982.

Morgan, William P. and Stephen E. Goldston, editors. *Exercise and Mental Health.* Washington: Hemisphere Publishing Corp., 1987.

Morse, Donald R., and Robert L. Pollack. *Nutrition, Stress and Aging: A Holistic Approach to the Relationships among Stress and Food Selection, Digestion, Nutrients, Body Weight, Disease and Longevity.* New York: AMS Press, 1988.

Orlandi, Mario, and Donald Prue with Annette Spence. *Encyclopedia of Good Health: Stress and Mental Health.* New York: Facts on File, 1989. (YA)

Young, Bettie B. *Stress in Children: How to Recognize, Avoid and Overcome It.* New York: Arbor House, 1985.

INDEX

ABOUT THE AUTHOR

Janet Bode specializes in writing nonfiction books for teenagers. Across the country, she asks students about the critical issues they face today. Then, to find guidance for the problems the students raise, she interviews professionals and experts on these specific topics. The result is a series of hard-hitting, award-winning books that combine revealing, teen-life stories with perceptive analysis and workable solutions.

The titles of these Watts publications include *Kids Having Kids: The Unwed Teenage Parent; Different Worlds: Interracial and Cross-Cultural Dating; New Kids on the Block: Oral Histories of Immigrant Teens,* a 1989 ALA Best Book for Young Adults, and *The Voices of Rape.*

A lifelong traveler, Ms. Bode has lived and worked in the United States, Europe, and Mexico. She now resides in New York City, where she is a member of the Authors Guild, PEN, and the Popular Culture Association.